# muscle Fords!

Edited by Thomas E. Bonsall

Osceola, Wisconsin 54020, USA ®

Bookman Publishing

Baltimore, Maryland

Printed in the U.S.A.


ISBN 0-934780-52-8

First Edition
First Printing



Inquiries may be directed to:
Bookman Dan!, Inc.
P.O. Box 13492
Baltimore, Maryland 21203

Book trade distribution by:
Motorbooks International
P. O. Box 2
Osceola, Wisconsin 54020

# Contents

# Loose on the Street! Ford High Performance Engines.

By Robert C. Ackerson

To anyone who reached adolescence during the years from 1932 to 1955 and had the typical American teenager's interest in automobiles, the V-8 engine was synonymous with Ford. Other manufacturers produced V-8s of course and most of them beat Ford to the showroom with overhead valve models. But in terms of sheer numbers, nobody built V-8s like Ford did. Nor, for that matter, did anyone else build V-8s that, thanks to their availability and straightforward design, were destined to become the backbone of the American hot rod movement. Chevrolet could introduce the Corvette with a six-cylinder engine and no one thought much about it. After all, what else could you expect from Chevrolet? But with Ford it was different. No one in their right mind could have envisioned a Thunderbird powered by a hopped-up "Mileage Maker Six."

The engineering, development and production of engines has always been an ambitious and expensive

**Ford division** Engine Cid, Carb, Code, Horsepower

| | 1960 | 1961 | 1962 | 1963 | 1964 |
|---|---|---|---|---|---|
| FALCON | | | | 260-2V(F) 164Bhp → | → |
| | | | | | |
| FAIRLANE TORINO | | | 221-2V(L) 145Bhp → | → | |
| | | | 260-2V(F) 164Bhp → | → | → |
| | | | | 289-2V(C) 195Bhp → | → |
| | | | | 289-4V HP(K) 271Bhp → | → |
| | | | | | |
| | | | | | |
| | | | | | 427-4V(W) 410Bhp → |
| | | | | | 427-8V(R) 425Bhp → |
| MUSTANG | | | | | |
| THUNDERBIRD | 352-2V(X) 235Bhp | 390-4V(Z) 300Bhp → | → | → | → |
| | 352-4V(Y) 300Bhp | 390-4V(Z) 375Bhp | | | |
| | | 390-6V(Z) 401Bhp | 390-6V(M) 401Bhp | 390-6V(M) 340Bhp | |
| FORD | | | | 260-2V(F) 164Bhp | |
| | | | | 289-2V(C) 195Bhp → | → |
| | | | | | |
| | 352-2V(X) 235Bhp | 352-2V(X) 220Bhp → | → | → | 352-4V(X) 250Bhp → |
| | 352-4V(Y) 300Bhp | 390-4V(Z) 300Bhp → | → | → | → |
| | 352-4V(Y) 360Bhp | 390-4V(Z) 375Bhp | 406-4V(B) 385Bhp → | → | |
| | | 390-6V(Z) 401Bhp | 406-6V(G) 405Bhp → | → | |
| | | | 390-4V HP(Q) 375Bhp | 427-4V(Q) 410Bhp → | → |
| | | | | 427-8V(R) 425Bhp → | → |

undertaking and Ford, obviously wishing to get the most for its design dollars, would often use one basic V-8 to create a family of engines for various applications. For example, derivatives of the original Ford V-8 included the 60 hp version, the 59A block used in prewar Ford trucks and postwar Ford cars as well as the original Lincoln-Zephyr V-12.

With its first ohv V-8, which debuted in 1954 in a 239 cid 130 hp form, Ford introduced the Y family of engines. With this modest horsepower rating and displacement, the Y-block V-8 didn't exactly eclipse Chevrolet, which that year drew 125 hp from its veteran 235.5 cid Blue Flame Six. But with the introduction of the Thunderbird in late 1954, followed by the full line of 1955 Fords, the Y-block V-8 family grew substantially. A 272 cid version was initially the largest V-8 available for the full-size Fords. In power pack form (8.5:1 cylinder heads, four-barrel carburetor, special intake manifold, vacuum timing, high-capacity radiator and dual exhausts), it developed 182 hp at 4600 rpm and 268 lb-ft of torque at 2600 rpm. Pushed off stride by the potency of Chevrolet's new, high-revving 265 cid V-8, Ford added the 292 cid Thunderbird V-8 to the regular Ford option list late in the year. Its respective horsepower ratings with manual or automatic transmission were 193 and 198 hp.

The ferocity with which Ford and Chevrolet pursued their respective performance images in 1955 set the stage for even more dramatic developments during the following year. Ford's opening salvo was led by the 292 Thunderbird with 202 hp. However, this was quickly supplanted by a more potent 205 hp "high-out" version. Compared to the 1955 version, this V-8 featured a higher lift cam, stronger rocker arms and a combustion chamber that retained a wedge shape but was revamped to provide more turbulence.

Even though the 205 hp engine could move a Ford sedan from zero to 60 mph in under 9 seconds, its reign as the most powerful Ford engine option was short-lived as the largest (312 cubic inches) member of the Y

| 1965 | 1966 | 1967 | 1958 | 1969 | 1970 |
|---|---|---|---|---|---|
| 289-2V(C) 200Bhp → | → | → | 289-2V(C) 195Bhp | 302-2V(F) 210Bhp | 302-2V(F) 220Bhp |
| | | 289-4V(A) 225Bhp | 302-4V(J) 235Bhp | | |
| | | | | | |
| 289-4V(A) 225Bhp | | 289-4V(A) 225Bhp | 302-2V(F) 210Bhp → | → | 302-2V(F) 220Bhp |
| 289-2V(C) 200Bhp → | → | → | 289-2V(C) 195Bhp | 351-2V(H) 250Bhp → | → |
| → | REGULAR FUEL—MANUAL TRANSMISSION 390-2V(Y) 265Bhp | 390-2V(Y) 270Bhp | 390-2V(Y) 265Bhp | 351-4V(M) 290Bhp | 351-4V(M) 300Bhp |
| | Reg. Fuel-Auto. Trans. 390-2V(H) 275Bhp | 390-4V(Z) 315Bhp | HYD. CAM 427-4V(W) 390Bhp | | 429-BOSS(Z) 375Bhp |
| | 390-4V GT(S) 335Bhp | 390-4V GT(S) 320Bhp | 390-4V GT(S) 325Bhp | 390-4V IP(S) 320Bhp | 429-4V(H) 360Bhp |
| → | → | → | 428-4V CJ(Q) 335Bhp | | 429-4V CJ(C) 370Bhp |
| → | → | → | RAM AIR 428-4V CJ(R) 335Bhp → | → | RAM AIR 429-4V CJ(J) 370Bhp |
| 260-2V(F) 164Bhp | | | | 302-2V(F) 210Bhp | 302-2V(F) 220Bhp |
| 289-2V(C) 200Bhp → | → | → | 289-2V(C) 195Bhp | 302-BOSS(G) 290Bhp → | → |
| 289-4V(A) 225Bhp → | → | → | 302-4V(J) 235Bhp | 351-2V(H) 250Bhp → | → |
| 289-4V HP(K) 271Bhp → | → | → | → | 351-4V(M) 290Bhp | 351-4V(M) 300Bhp |
| | | 390-4V GT(S) 320Bhp | 390-4V GT(S) 325Bhp | 390-4V IP(S) 320Bhp | |
| | | | 428-4V CJ(Q) 335Bhp → | → | → |
| | | | RAM AIR 428-4V CJ(R) 335Bhp → | → | → |
| | | | HYD. CAM 427-4V(W) 390Bhp | 429-BOSS(Z) 375Bhp → | → |
| → | 390-4V(Z) 315Bhp → | → | → | | |
| | | | | | |
| | 428-4V(Q) 345Bhp → | → | 429-4V(N) 360Bhp → | → | → |
| | | | | | |
| 289-2V(C) 200Bhp → | → | → | 302-2V(F) 210Bhp → | → | 302-2V(F) 220Bhp |
| | | 289-4V HP(K) 271Bhp | | | 351-2V(H) 250Bhp |
| → | → | | | | |
| → | 390-4V(Z) 315Bhp → | → | → | | |
| | REG. FUEL 390-2V(Y) 265Bhp | PREM. FUEL 390-2V(X) 280Bhp → | → | REG. FUEL—MANUAL & AUTO. TRANS. 390-2V(Y) 265Bhp → | → |
| | 428-4V(Q) 345Bhp → | → | → | 429-2V(K) 320Bhp → | → |
| | 427-4V(W) 410Bhp → | → | HYD. CAM 427-4V(W) 390Bhp | 429-4V(N) 360Bhp → | → |
| → | → | → | | | |

V-8 family. It became Ford's main assault weapon for the NASCAR Grand National wars. With an 8.4:1 compression ratio, five main bearings and a single Holley four-barrel, its maximum horsepower was 225 at 4600 rpm with Fordomatic. Before the era of direct factory participation came to a close in 1957, Ford was offering this engine as the Thunderbird Special Supercharged V-8. Available to the public as a $447.60 option, it developed 300 hp at 4800 rpm. An 8.5:1 compression ratio was specified. The supercharger was a Paxton centrifugal type. This 300 hp rating was generally regarded as conservative, since 340 hp was claimed for the NASCAR version.

Ford's involvement with really large displacement V-8s began in 1958, when the first FE V-8 engine (standard in the four-seater Thunderbird) became available as the Interceptor V-8 (332 cubic inches, and either 240 or 265 hp) or the Interceptor 352 Special V-8 with 300 hp, and 10.2:1 compression ratio.

The FE's debut in these forms was somewhat inauspicious, since both were at best regarded as mild performers. However, the basic FE block would be bored and stroked into the 390HP in 1961, which in turn would evolve into the 406 cid V-8 in 1962 and the 427 cid V-8 the following year.

The opening of the new Daytona International Speedway in 1959 initiated a new era of high-speed stock car racing. This was a development that Ford could not afford to ignore and with Donald Frey, the executive engineer of Ford Division product planning eager to get Ford back into racing, the introduction of a potent new Interceptor engine the same month as Daytona's debut was far from coincidental. Furthermore, the arrival of Lee Iacocca as the general manager of the Ford Division was just over the horizon and his tenure would be marked by a strong emphasis upon youth, speed and racing. The peak outputs of this 352 cid engine were 360 hp at 6000 rpm and 380 lb-ft of torque at 3400 rpm. Key design features included mechanical

## what is an engine family

An engine "family" is a group of engines that have evolved from one basic design. The "FE" Family, for instance, came on the scene in 1958 as the 332 - 352 CID engines. They were designed to produce more power and replace the "Y" block V-8's that reached their ultimate form as the 292 - 312 CID engines in the late fifties. The "FE" Family did this, of course, in later improved versions that included the 390 - 406 - 428 and the all-out high performance 427 mill.

Component design within an engine family may differ . . . as may certain dimensions such as bore and stroke to give us the popular cubic inch displacement and horsepower ratings to distinguish between engines. Many parts from an engine "family" are, however, identical or at least interchangeable. Maintaining certain key block dimensions makes this possible. Exceptions exist, but generally an engine family has the same center-to-center distance on cylinder bore spacing (which can mean a common crankshaft) . . . and head bolt pattern (which can mean common cylinder heads) . . . and the same dimension from crankshaft centerline to top of the block (which can mean common connecting rod lengths, possibly interchangeable pistons and various valve train parts.)

Important dimensions are shown with the specifications at the beginning of each engine family section. It is keyed to these drawings to indicate their location.

The following chart shows the engine CID for several engine families. This book only covers the last four.

**KEY**

- A Bore
- B Stroke
- C Bore Spacing
- D Crank Main Journal Dia.
- E Crank Rod Journal Dia.
- F Cam Journal Dia.
- G ℄ of Crank to Top of Block (Head Face)
- H Block Deck Height Clearance
- I Piston Compression Height
- J Con Rod ctr-to-ctr Length
- K Valve Head Dia.
- L Valve Stem Dia.
- M Spring Height

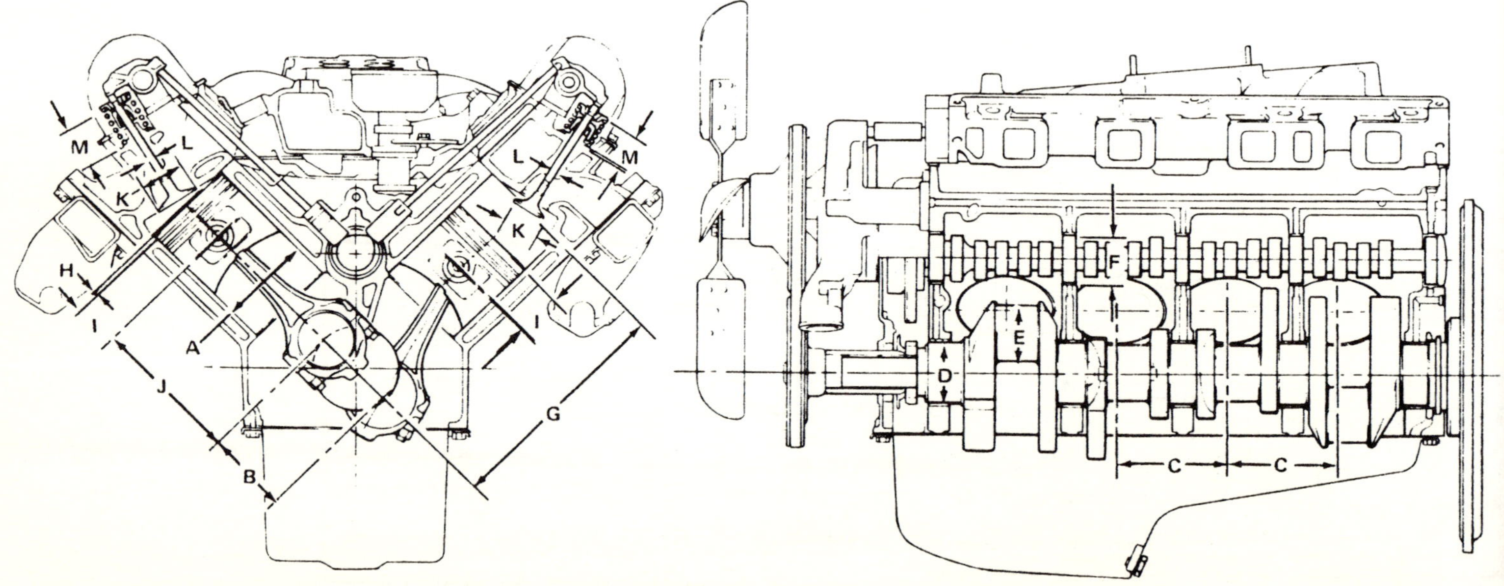

lifters, 10.6:1 compression ratio pistons, an aluminum intake manifold, drop-forged rather than cast exhaust valves, dual ignition points and a 540 cfm Holley four-barrel carburetor.

Common to all 352 engines was a modular iron crankshaft, but the crank for the 360 hp version had increased bearing clearances to improve oil flow. The heads for both 332 and 352 cid FE engines had identical valve head diameters of 2.03 inches (intake) and 1.56 inches (exhaust).

After three years of unchanged cubic inch displacement, the 352 FE engine was expanded to 390 cubic inches in 1961, due to a 4.05 inch rather than 4.00 inch bore. A mild version, the Thunderbird 390 Special V-8 with 300 hp at 4600 rpm was offered, but the really interesting forms were the Police Interceptor V-8 with 330 hp at 5000 rpm and the 375 hp Thunderbird 390 Super V-8, which Ford also identified as the 390 High Performance V-8. Both types had mechanical cams, forged steel connecting rods, modular iron connecting rods providing for a 3.78-inch stroke and a heavier harmonic balance to counteract harmonics at higher revs. Enhancing reliability were modifications that included stronger block webbing, main bearing caps, revised oil galleys and pressure relief valve. An improved aluminum intake manifold with 10 percent larger passages was used, along with a bigger 600 cfm Holley four-barrel carburetor. Ford also took pains to maintain a high level of quality control for the 375 hp engines. All cylinder blocks were carefully examined to ferret out any with weak spots. Pistons for the 390HP were regular production units, but they were first selected for size before being x-rayed to determine any possible flaws.

Although the official horsepower rating of the 390HP was 375 at 6000 rpm, it was possible for a carefully assembled version to come very close to a horsepower-per-cubic-inch output.

Late in the 1960 calendar year, Ford released a dealer-installed option of an aluminum intake manifold sporting three Holley two-barrel carburetors. The center unit had a 240 cfm rating with the outer models credited with a 300 cfm capability. The result, according to Ford, was 401 hp at 6000 rpm and 430 lb-ft at 3500 rpm. One Ford with this setup barely lost a trophy at the 1961 NHRA Winter Nationals with a run of 105.50 mph and 13.33 seconds.

Ford described the 406 cid V-8 of 1962 and 1963 as the "first of the big winners." Beyond any doubt it ranks in Ford history as the engine that made Ford a serious force in drag and oval track competition. From a design viewpoint, the 406 engine represented the halfway mark in the development of the 390 engine into the 427. Its block was identical to that of the 390 High Performance except that it was bored an additional 0.080 inches, from 4.05 inches to 4.13 inches.

Two versions, both introduced in December, 1961, were available. With a single 600 cfm carburetor, peak horsepower was 385 at 5800 rpm. Maximum torque was 444 lb-ft at 3400 rpm. Use of the triple, two-barrel carburetor setup (now with a 920 cfm rating) provided 405 hp at 5800 rpm and 448 lb-ft at 3500 rpm. All 1962 and early 1963 406 blocks used conventional 2-bolt main bearing caps, but a few late 1963 engines carried cross-bolted caps for the No. 2, 3 and 4 main bearings. The crankshaft was cast from nodular iron with .12-inch grooves in each main journal for additional oil supply as found on the 390HP engine. Also shared with

**1962 Ford Galaxie 500 Sunliner**

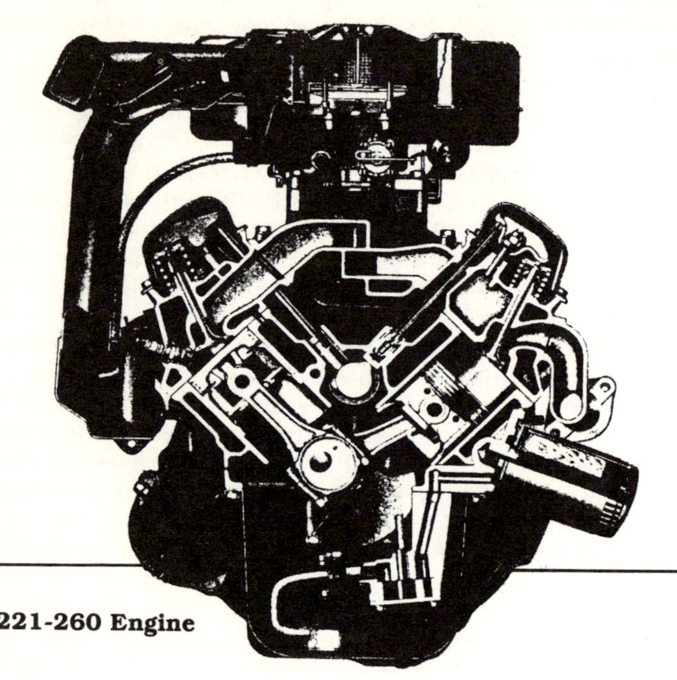

**221-260 Engine**

the 390HP were the 406 engine's forged steel connecting rods. They were, however, somewhat heavier and thus required larger counterweights. While the 390HP was fitted with "eyebrowed" top aluminum pistons, those found on the 406 were of "flat top" design, providing for a 10.9:1 compression ratio. The cylinder heads of the 406 carried the same 2.03 inch intake valves as the 390HP, but had larger 1.66-inch exhaust valves.

Ford began its Total Performance (which it defined as "the ability of a vehicle to fully accomplish its intended function") program in 1963 and the leading edge of that offensive, introduced as a 1963 .5 option, was the 427 engine. Ford regarded the 427 as the "ultimate wedge" and was justly proud of its ability to rev to 7000 rpm and to withstand 500 miles of high-speed banked oval racing.

Available for all full-size Fords except station wagons were two versions with either a single or dual four-barrel carburetors. The former was rated at 410 hp at 5600 rpm and 470 lb-ft at 3400 rpm. With twin 540 cfm Holleys, these figures rose to 425 hp at 6000 rpm and 480 lb-ft at 3700 rpm. Yet another alternative, intended exclusively for serious drag racing competition, had a 12:1 compression ratio, dual 600 cfm Holley carburetors and a long duration, 300o camshaft. This high riser engine used a cast-iron crank, stronger rods, lightweight valves, machined combustion chambers and pop-up pistons. All 427 blocks were cast from high strength alloy iron.

The largest FE engine, the 428 cid V-8 was first offered in 1966 with a mild hydraulic cam as the Thunderbird Special V-8. Its maximum horsepower was 345 at 4600 rpm. Ford readily admitted that it "didn't look like much of a performer . . . just a big block, hydraulic cammer with lots of torque to tool Thunderbirds around the street." However, that state of affairs was dramatically altered in the spring of 1968, when the 428-4V Cobra Jet version replaced the Cobra 427 V-8 as Ford's main performance engine.

It was easy to regard the 428 as a stroked 406, with its bore and stroke measurements of 4.13 inches and 3.98 inches. However, in terms of design, it had a close relationship to an expanded 390 cid V-8, due to its similar oiling system and 2-bolt main bearing caps. Whereas the Thunderbird 428-4V was fitted with standard 390-4V type connecting rods, the Cobra Jet version had Police Interceptor type rods, with stronger big ends and larger cap retaining bolts. The more powerful (360 hp at 5400 rpm to 335 hp at 5600 rpm) Super Cobra Jet used even beefier rods patterned after those of the 427 engine. When first introduced, the 428CJ carried a 785 cfm four-barrel carburetor on its cast-iron manifold (Police Interceptor 428 manifolds were aluminum). The following year (1969) the Cobra Jet was still rated at an admittedly conservative 335 hp, but at a lower 5200 rpm level. Revisions included a Holley 735 cfm four-barrel carb, larger ports and cast-iron exhaust headers. Also offered was a Ram Air option. All 428 engines had hydraulic lifters and dished cast aluminum pistons. Intake and exhaust valves measured 2.09 inches and 1.66 inches, respectively.

The introduction of the intermediate-sized Fairlane brought with it a new 221 cid V-8 which was destined to be the first of six very important members of the 90oV engine family. Those 221 cubic inches provided a modest 145 hp at 4400 rpm and 216 lb-ft at 2200 rpm. But by 1963, with a larger 3.80 (instead of 3.50) inch bore and the same 2.87-inch stroke of the 221 cid engine, this V-8 displaced 260 cubic inches. Horsepower was a respectable 164 at 4400 rpm and peak torque stood at 258 lb-ft at 2200 rpm. Further increases to 289 cubic inches in 1963 .5 and to 302 cubic inches in 1968 were accomplished by use of a larger 4.00 bore (1963 .5) and a 3.00 stroke (1968). Common to all versions was an ultra oversquare design which allowed the use of relatively large valves, and short connecting rods. The result was a very compact and rigid block, reduced piston speed and less friction. Making a major contribution to what were destined to become classic high performance V-8s was the thin-wall casting technique used for the 90oV engine's block and cylinder heads.

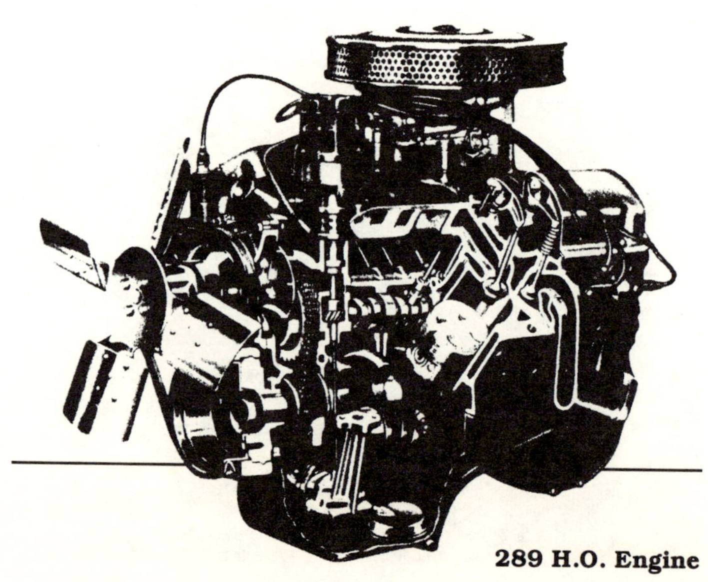

**289 H.O. Engine**

**351 Windsor Engine**

The first extra-strong 90oV was the 289HP, which was optional for 1963-65 Fairlanes, Comets and 1965-68 Mustangs. Its principal features included a solid lifter cam, a single 480 cfm four-barrel carburetor, cast, high strength, flat top pistons, high nodular iron crankshaft and forged steel connecting rods and exhaust valves. With an 11.0:1 compression ratio, its vital statistics were 271 hp at 6000 rpm and 312 lb-ft at 3400 rpm. All 90oV engines had a five main bearing crankshaft.

The 302 Boss engine, introduced for the Mustang in 1969, was modestly depicted by Ford as a "high output version of the standard 302 that has proven very competitive as a 5 litre F.I.A. Formula engine in Trans Am International Sedan Racing." In other words, it was a street edition of a road-racing engine! As was almost common practice, Ford credited the 302 Boss with respectable but definitely modest horsepower and torque outputs. Peak horsepower was placed at 290 at 5800 rpm, with 290 lb-ft of torque attained at 4300 rpm. Probably the most outstanding component of the 302 Boss was its polyangle wedge combustion chambers, which created high turbulence for more complete combustion and power. Furthermore, this design enabled canted valves to be used, which resulted in better breathing as gases flowed in a straighter line both leaving and entering the cylinders. The 1969 Boss 302 engines used intake valves with 2.23-inch heads, while those of the 1970 engine measured 2.19 inches. This seemingly retrogressive step actually improved performance by maintaining greater air flow at low rpms for better low-end response. Common to both versions was a forged steel crankshaft with 4-bolt main bearing caps at the No. 2, 3 and 4 journals, a solid lifter cam, plus specially hardened push rods. A free-breathing, high rise over/under aluminum intake manifold carried a 780 cfm, four-barrel carburetor. Rounding out the impressive credentials of the 302 Boss were forged steel connecting rods, pop-up forged aluminum 10.5:1 (nominal compression ratio) pistons, dual point distributor and an oil baffle in the pan.

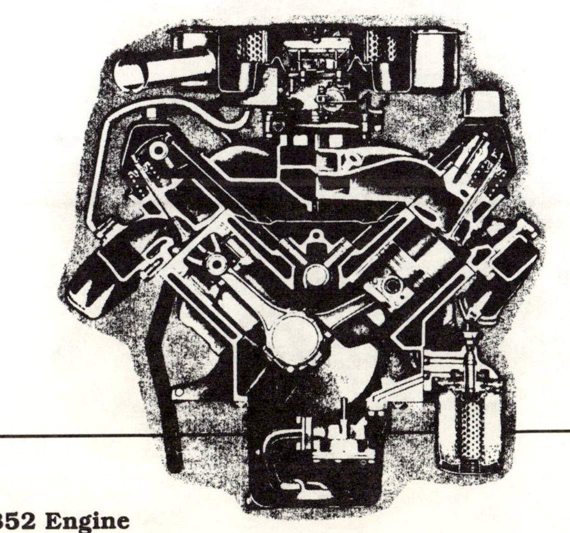

**352 Engine**

The largest and last member of the 90oV family was the 351 Windsor. Cast from different cores than the 289 and 302 engines, the 351 W deck was 1.275 inches higher to accommodate its longer 3.50-inch stroke. In addition, the 351 had thicker cylinder walls and stronger main bearing bulkheads.

Beginning in 1969, the 351 Windsor was used extensively by Ford. At various times it served as the standard engine for the Mustang Mach I and was available in combination with the Mustang's GT Equipment Group option as well as a power plant for intermediate and full-sized Fords.

"A family of one" was Ford's description of the 351 Cleveland. Whereas the 351 Windsor was the largest member of the 90oV family, the 351 Cleveland belonged to the 335 family. The Cleveland, with its polyangle combustion chambers, canted valves and rounded ports, bore a resemblance to Ford's NASCAR 429 engines and was often compared to the 302 Boss. However, few parts of the 351 Cleveland interchanged with the 302 Boss or, for that matter, with the 351 Windsor.

The 351 Cleveland was first available in 1970 in either two- or four-barrel carburetor form. Their respective horsepower ratings were 250 at 4600 rpm and 300 at 5400 rpm. The two-barrel version had a relatively mild 9.5:1 compression and a peak torque reading of 355 lb-ft at 2600 rpm. Clevelands with the four-barrel were credited with 380 lb-ft at 3400 rpm and an 11.9:1 compression ratio.

When the trend toward use of no-lead or low-lead fuel and the concurrent reduction of compression ratios began in 1971, the 351 Cleveland 4V still managed to turn out 285 hp at 5400 rpm with a 10.7:1 compression ratio. The 351 Cleveland also was offered as the Boss HO V-8. Its compression ratio remained a heady 11.0:1 and healthy outputs of 330 hp at 5400 rpm and 370 lb-ft of torque at 4000 rpm were claimed. Among the many virtues of the Boss HO were four-bolt main bearing caps, husky rods and pistons, a high nodular crank, mechanical lifters and a high lift cam.

In 1972, the Boss 351 was transformed into the 351 HO which, with a 9.2:1 compression ratio, was rated at 266 hp. For 1973 the most powerful Ford engine available was yet another 351 Cleveland variant, the 351CJ which, even with a 7.9:1 compression

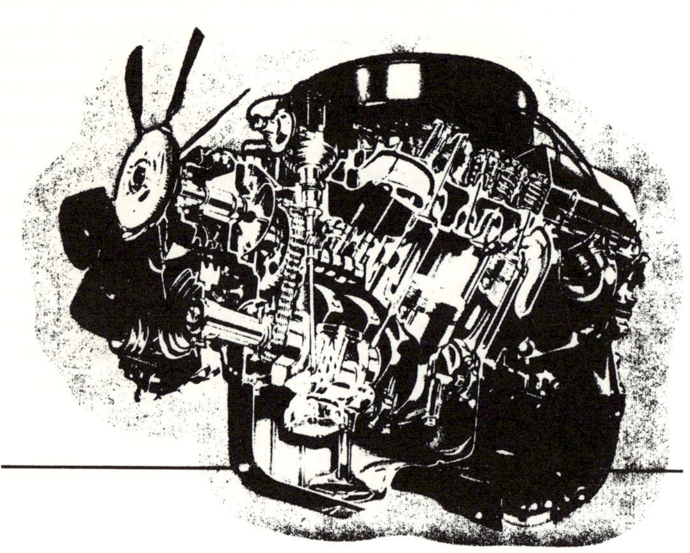

429 CJ-SCJ Engine

427 Engine

ratio, could master 259 hp at 5600 rpm.

Representing the culmination of Ford's experiences with both small and big block engines were the four members of the 385 engine family. Ford emphasized that while they featured lightweight, skirtless blocks like the 90oV engines and had displacements and power ratings within the range of the FE V-8s, the 385 family engines were far more than just hybrids of those two sets. Instead, Ford liked to talk about their canted valves and very large rounded ports that represented the 385 engine's forte of functioning as a high-torquing, low-emission engine for general passenger car use that was easily adoptable for successful high-performance operation.

The first version of the 385 family, the "Thunder Jet" 429, was introduced in 1968 with either a two- or four-barrel carburetor. The following year a 460 cid version was introduced for the Lincoln Continental. It was very similar to the Thunder Jet, except for a longer 3.85-inch rather than 3.59-inch stroke.

Beginning with the 1970 model year, the 429 was offered as either the 429 Cobra Jet or 429 Super Cobra Jet. The former was essentially a 429 Thunder Jet with a 760 cfm Rochester Quadra-Jet carburetor, dual plane cast-iron manifold and stronger components, such as a higher nodularity content crankshaft and a hydraulic cam. Its maximum horsepower was 370 at 5400 rpm, while peak torque output was 450 lb-ft at 3400 rpm. Nominal compression ratio was 10.7:1.

While Ford described the 429CJ as a "medium performance 'street' machine," the Super Cobra Jet was depicted as the engine for the "serious competitor." It used the same intake manifold as the CJ, but was equipped with a 780 cfm 4V carburetor. Both engines shared the same type of connecting rods but the

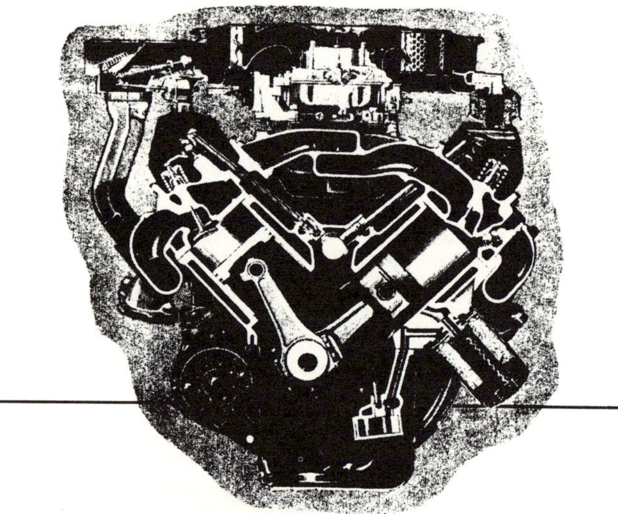

429-460 Engine

390-410 Engine

Super Cobra Jet had forged aluminum pistons of the same design as the cast aluminum versions used for the CJ. Also found on the Super Cobra Jet was a mechanical cam, four-bolt main bearings and an oil cooler. Although both had identical power ratings, there was little doubt that the Super Cobra Jet was considerably stronger than its official power levels.

The most extreme version of the 429 was its Boss version, of which Ford noted: "There's no hiding what (it) was designed for." In other words, this was an engine whose sole reason for existence was NASCAR racing domination, which required a production version. The initial 279 engines produced were available only with hydraulic lifters. The subsequent engine had different rods and pistons and were supplied with either hydraulic or mechanical lifters. Horsepower and torque ratings were obviously understated: 375 hp at 5200 rpm and 450 lb-ft at 3400 rpm.

The 429 Boss block was similar to that of other 429 engines, save for revised castings. Except for the number five journal, four-bolt main bearing caps were used. Perhaps the most outstanding features of the 429 Boss were the lightweight aluminum cylinder heads with their crescent combustion chambers. Intake valves measured 2.28 inches, while exhausts were of a 1.905-inch diameter. A dual plane, over/under, aluminum intake manifold was used on all 429 Boss engines. A 735 cfm four-barrel Holley was also fitted.

It's unlikely that we'll ever see engines the likes of which made Ford one of America's premier performance cars of the golden age of power. But in the form of the Mustang GT's potent V-8, their spirit lives on. With big displacements and soaring power peaks, they took us to new heights of automotive excitement that were almost unbelievable then and unforgettable now.

# AND IT'S COUSIN "the cammer"

## 427 single over-head cam (SOHC)

Mustang 2+2 with Cobra Jet 428-cubic-inch V-8 during Hot Rod Magazine performance tests.

# "Hot Rod" Sees the Light

**"The Cobra Jet will be the utter delight of every Ford lover and the bane of all the rest because, quite frankly, it is the fastest running Pure Stock in the history of man."**

**HOT ROD MAGAZINE**
**March, 1968**

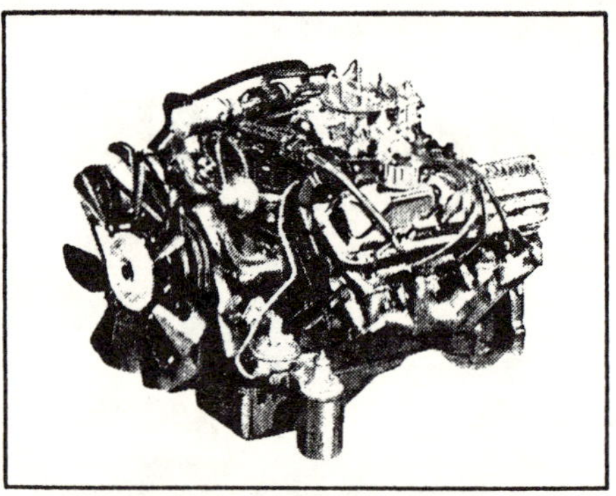

## Ford introduces the 428-cu.in. Cobra Jet V-8

With some 36 years of experience behind them in making strong, relatively lightweight big bore blocks, Ford's performance-minded engineers set out to build the Cobra Jet. They took the bottom end and beefed it up with the 428-cubic-inch Police Interceptor V-8, high pressure oil pump and large diameter con-rod bolts.

On the top end they dipped into the barrel of Ford race-track goodies. Cylinder heads are straight from the trophy-winning 427 Series 1 engine. Compression ratio was pegged at 10.7 to 1 and quiet hydraulic lifters open the oversize valves.

With a bore and stroke of 4.13 by 3.98 inches, the Cobra Jet develops 335 hp at 5400 and produces 440 lbs-ft of wall-climbing torque. The carburetor is a special new 2-float, 4-barrel Holley and exhaust headers are of special low-restriction design.

That's it. Cobra Jet 428. What it does for Mustang GT's in the 0-60 mph run will make your eyeballs click! It's on the production line right now. The performance option for all Fairlanes, Torinos, and Mustang GT's. Immediate delivery. All you do is order it . . . and GO!

**RESULTS OF HOT ROD MAGAZINE TESTS**

**Vehicle:** Mustang Cobra Jet

**Performance**

| | |
|---|---|
| 0-30 | 3.0 seconds |
| 0-40 | 3.4 seconds |
| 0-50 | 5.0 seconds |
| 0-60 | 5.9 seconds |

Standing quarter-mile . . . . . 106.64 mph in 13.56 seconds

**See the light—the switch is on to Ford!**

Ford ...has a better idea.

# Put Cobra venom in your V-8!

## Cobra Kits full of power and pizzazz for Ford 221, 260 or 289 blocks.

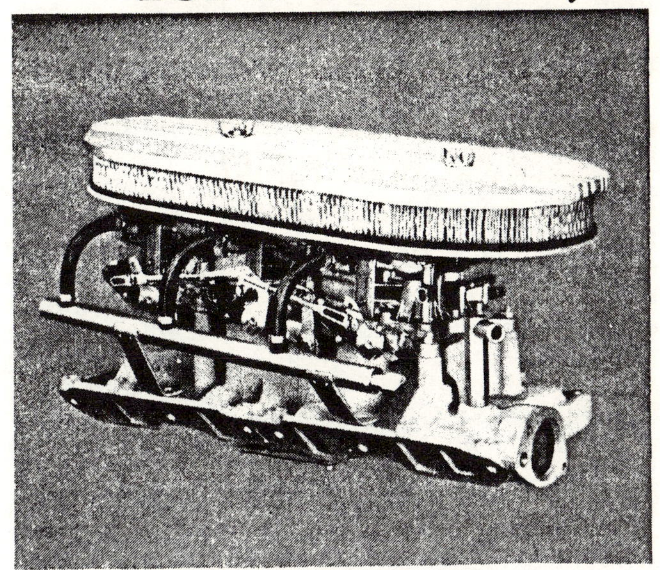

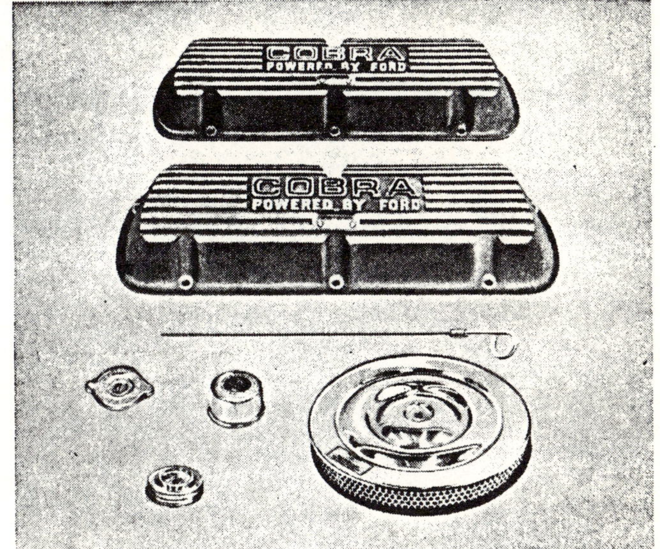


**THREE 2-V INDUCTION KIT.** Use this kit with the distributor, cam, and cylinder head kits and watch the horses soar! Kit has three 2-V carburetors on cast aluminum intake manifold, special air cleaner. Mechanical linkage lets you "go on one" for economy, use the others for maximum go. Cobra medallions included. Part #C4OZ-6B068-A (260 CID), C4OZ-6B068-B (289). Each $212.55*

**ENGINE DRESS-UP KIT.** Adds a racy "Cobra" look to your engine. This stylish kit includes finned, polished aluminum valve covers; long-lasting chrome dip stick, radiator cap, master cylinder cap, oil filler cap, air cleaner cover and filter. 1963 kit fits 221, 260 and 289 Ford V-8 blocks; '64 kit fits 260 and 289 engines. Part #C3OZ-6980-A ('63)—$72.45*, #C4OZ-6980-A ('64). $78.35*

**SINGLE 4-V INDUCTION KIT.** This 4-V will give you greater performance without drastic modification of your mill. Kit has intake manifold, air cleaner, 4-V carburetor, required gaskets, necessary hardware. Cobra Medallions included. Part #C4OZ-6B068-D. $122.60*

**CAM KIT.** This kit has been specially engineered with correct tolerances for Ford 221, 260, 289 blocks. Consists of finely machined camshaft and 16 tappets and is the same type used in winning Cobras. Kit includes Cobra medallions. Part #C4OZ-6A257-A. $75.10*

**DISTRIBUTOR KIT.** This high-performance kit consists of heavy-duty distributor and leads. Features dual points, centrifugal spark advance. Use the kit to give your engine the high-speed performance characteristics you want that are especially suited for drag strip operations and other high RPM requirements. Part #C4DZ-12050-A. $49.80*

**DUAL EXHAUST KIT.** For converting standard exhaust systems to dual system. This kit includes pipe, necessary hardware, and two straight-through 4-inch glass-pack mufflers to give you better performance and increased horsepower ratings. Part #C4DZ-5210-A. $69.95*

*Manufacturer's suggested retail price. Installation charges and state and local taxes, if any, are extra.

PRODUCTS OF Ford MOTOR COMPANY

**These are just a sample of the Cobra Kits you can get from your Ford Dealer.**

# Birds in the Bush: Thunderbird, 1955-1982.

By Robert C. Ackerson

At almost any point in time since its debut at the Detroit Automobile Show on February 20, 1954, automotive journalists have never been lacking for words to describe the Ford Thunderbird.

In over 30 years of production, the T-Bird has been controversial, a trend setter, available in two- and four-passenger form as well as in two- and four-door versions and, most importantly (especially to Ford), an extremely popular automobile.

Much of the discussion about the original Thunderbird evolved around the type of car it really was. Sports car enthusiasts of the mid-fifties, manifesting the worst consequences of automotive inbreeding, tended to regard Detroit as incapable of producing an automobile that could cover winding roads fairly rapidly and be really fun to drive. Ford didn't exactly help the Thunderbird's status among members of the clan by first describing it as "a completely new kind of sports car" and then deciding to call it a "personal luxury car." In yet another change of mind, an October, 1954 advertisement of the Thunderbird had described it as "a new kind of personal car that combines sports car styling and performance with passenger car conveniences." After testing the 1955 model, "Road & Track" (March, 1955) noted that "the Ford Motor Co. refrains from calling this car a sports car, but we think this policy is being overly cautious. The Thunderbird is a touring sports car." But a year later, in its August, 1956 issue, "Road & Track" backed off from this assessment, noting in regard to the 1956 model that "this is no sports car by any stretch of the imagination."

In the real world, this type of philosophical discourse mattered little. The two-seater T-Bird possessed appeal in abundance, easily outselling its arch-rival from Chevrolet, demonstrating impressive acceleration, more than adequate handling and a look that is still appealing after three decades.

With a trim 102-inch wheelbase, 175.3-inch overall length and a height (from ground level to the highest point of its removable fiberglass top) of 52.2 inches, the Thunderbird's proportions were near perfect for a two-seater. Its styling was closely related to that of the full-size Ford, but there never was any possibility of confusing one for the other! Thunderbirds were a breed apart in that respect, even though some body components, such as taillights, were interchangeable with other Ford automobiles.

Only one engine, Ford's 292 cid V-8 was available for the first T-Bird. If Fordomatic was ordered, this V-8, with 8.5:1 compression ratio, developed 198 hp at 4400 rpm and 286 lb-ft of torque at 2500 rpm. Those with either overdrive or the standard three-speed manual gearbox had a slightly lower 8.1:1 compression ratio and a reduced rating of 193 hp at 4400 rpm. Both engines had a single Holley four-barrel carburetor. More than offsetting its slight power disadvantage

**1955 Thunderbird**

**1956 Thunderbird**

were the close ratios of the manual transmission Thunderbird. A 2.32:1 first gear and 1.48:1 second gear were employed.

If the Thunderbird's suspension didn't elicit rave reviews from observers who liked to flaunt their knowledge of deDion rear axles and all-independent springing, it was at the least a prime example of mid-fifties American design thought. At the front were ball joints (first used by Ford in 1952), coil springs, a stabilizer bar and double-acting shock absorbers. At the rear, semi-elliptic five-leaf springs were employed with inserts at the tips of all leaves. Wind-up bumpers, double-acting shocks and tension-type rear shackles were also used. The result was a very successful blending of safe and stable cornering power sufficient for spirited but noncompetitive driving and riding qualities that were among the best available from any contemporary sports car.

Thunderbirds always seemed to weigh more than expected and even these early two-seaters, ready for the open road, weighed over 3,600 pounds. However, with nearly 200 hp on tap, they could cover any road rather rapidly. With standard rear axles of 3.73:1 (standard three-speed), 3.92:1 (overdrive) or 3.30:1 (Fordomatic), the Thunderbird moved quickly away from a standing start. Zero to 60 mph required less than 10 seconds and the quarter-mile was covered in a respectable 17 seconds. In good tune, the Thunderbird could reach a 112 mph top speed without difficulty. An interesting after-market option for the Thunderbird was McCulloch's variable speed supercharger. Its manufacturer claimed it boosted peak horsepower up to 260 and yielded a zero to 60 mph time of a mere six seconds. Zero to 100 mph was accomplished in just 16 seconds and a dazzling top speed of 131 mph was possible.

Although one owner complained that "I have been disappointed in the top speed of 110 miles per hour," 61 percent of the respondents to "Popular Mechanic's" survey of 1955 Thunderbird owners rated the T-Bird's power and performance as its best-liked feature. In second place, with a 46 percent rating, was the Thunderbird's handling, followed closely by styling (45 percent).

At Daytona's February, 1955, Speed Week, the Thunderbirds demonstrated plenty of punch as one, driven by Bill Spear, won the under-$4,000 Sports Car Class with a two-way average speed of 121.992 mph. In second place was another Thunderbird at 121.826 mph. This was only the beginning of several days of triumph by T-Birds that clearly humiliated not only the Corvette, but also the highly regarded Jaguar XK and Mercedes 300SL models. On February 22, the Thunderbird averaged 124.633 mph to win the American Sports Car Class. In yet another impressive demonstration of its ability, a T-Bird finished second to a 4.9 Ferrari in the standing start mile competition for unlimited sports cars. The Ford's average of 84.66 mph compared extremely favorably with the best 300SL's mark of 81.91 mph.

With an East Coast base price of $3,278, the first Thunderbird was competitively priced with other cars (with room for either two or more occupants) that offered comparable performance and features. In this regard, the T-Bird's list of standard equipment needed no apologies. Among the items listed were a tachometer, electric clock with sweep second hand, power seat, fiberglass top (the convertible top was offered for $290.00 or $75.00 in lieu of the hard top), dual exhausts, dual horns and all-vinyl trim.

With a production run of 16,155 cars for the 1955 model year, the Thunderbird was obviously a success from the moment the first example was constructed on September 9, 1954. However, if the controversy about the Thunderbird's status as a sports car had been live-

**Following pages, 1957 Thunderbird**

1957

1958 Thunderbird

1959 Thunderbird

1960 Thunderbird

1961 Thunderbird

1962 Thunderbird

1963 Thunderbird

Following pages, 1964 Thunderbird

**1965 Thunderbird**

ly, it paled beside the uproar that greeted the restyled 1956 version. Today, any of the two-seater Birds are coveted collectibles, but in 1956 there were many who believed Ford had needlessly changed the Thunderbird's appearance and that the result was not an improvement. The use of an externally-mounted spare tire in continental style added 10 inches of overall length and, while appealing in some respects, was really not appropriate on a contemporary automobile. An interesting no-cost option was the twin circular porthole feature for the removable hardtop. Two other easily detected features of the 1956 Thunderbird were the front fender positioned vent doors and the wind wings for the front doors. Other changes for 1956 included a revised hood insignia, reshaped headlight trim, taillight lenses and frames, exhaust pipes (which now exited through the bumpers) and the removal of the crossed flag insignia from the fuel filler lid. The absence of the same logo from the Thunderbird's hood had implications beyond serving as a simple example of a mild styling face-lift. By the time the 1956 Thunderbird was entering production, Ford had digested the results of a major survey of 1955 T-Bird owners by its Market Research Group. Essentially, the response boiled down to an interest in a new model with seating for four passengers, additional luggage room, easier entry and exit, and improved accommodations. In other words, they wanted an automobile that remained a spirited performer but not at the expense of traditional American automotive features.

With both Ford and Chevrolet busy stuffing ever more powerful and larger engines into their sedans, it was natural that the Thunderbird would receive a similar dose of medicine. Thus the top engine for the 1956 Birds equipped with Fordomatic was the 312 cid V-8 with a 9.25:1 compression ratio, 225 hp at 4600 rpm and 324 lb-ft of torque at 2600 rpm. Models with overdrive had the same engine but with an 8.4:1 compression ratio and slightly lower ratings of 215 hp at 4600 rpm and 289 lb-ft at 2600 rpm. The smaller 292 cid V-8 was reserved for the few Thunderbirds equipped with a three-speed manual gearbox. Its horsepower with an 8.4:1 compression ratio was 202 at 4600 rpm. Peak torque was 289 lb-ft at 2600 rpm. All three engines were fitted with single Holley four-barrel carburetors. The net result was slightly improved performance. For example, "Road and Track" (August, 1956) reported a zero to 60 mph time of 9.3 seconds with its Fordomatic T-Bird test car.

Since the Thunderbird was closely patterned along the design lines of the full-size Fords and Mercurys, it was not difficult to improve its road performance by some simple component transplants. For example, the Thunderbird's stock front springs were rated at 290 lb/in. and it was a minor task to install those from the large Ford sedans which, at 360 lb/in., were quite a bit stiffer. At the rear, a firmer suspension could be achieved by adding additional leaf springs. To improve braking performance, it was possible to install larger brake units from either a 1956 Mercury or Lincoln.

The two-seater Thunderbird was dramatically and handsomely restyled for 1957. The increase in production from 15,631 in 1956 to 21,380 for the 1957 model year is one measurement of the success of this revision. The twin, bullet-shaped, spinner-type bumper guards, that could be traced back to the 1951 Ford, were replaced by far more slender and shapely formed units cast integrally into the bumper. The grille, now fully exposed, was somewhat higher than on previous models. Equally prominent was the Thunderbird's new, longer by nearly 5.5 inches, rear deck. In tune with the styling of the all-new 1957 big Fords were canted fins whose leading edge extended into the front door region. The use of 14- inch, instead of 15-inch, wheels also gave the new Thunderbird a lower profile.

Although Chevrolet and the Corvette were getting plenty of justified attention with their 283 cid fuel-injected V-8 and its one horsepower per cubic inch output, the changes made in the Thunderbird's engine lineup were also substantial. The base engine for use

1966 Thunderbird

1967 Thunderbird

1968 Thunderbird

Following pages, 1969 Thunderbird

1969

**1970 Thunderbird**

with the standard three-speed manual gearbox, the Thunderbird 292 V-8 was equipped with a single two-barrel carburetor, and with a 9.1:1 compression ratio, developed 212 hp at 4500 rpm. If either Fordomatic or overdrive was ordered, the Thunderbird 312 Special V-8 was installed. A single Holley four-barrel carburetor and 9.1:1 compression ratio provided 245 hp at 4500 rpm. The 312 cid engine was also available as the Thunderbird 312 Super V-8 with either 270 or 285 horsepower. Both had 9.7:1 compression ratios and twin Holley four-barrels. The latter version was fitted with a NASCAR racing cam and developed its peak power at 5000 rpm compared to 4800 rpm for the 270 hp V-8.

Rarest of the 1957 Thunderbirds was the supercharged "F" model, of which only slightly more than 200 were produced. These were equipped with model VR-57 McCulloch variable ratio superchargers and a single Holley four-barrel carburetor. With an 8.5:1 compression ratio, maximum horsepower was 300 at 4800 rpm.

Two of the most potent factory-sponsored Thunderbirds ever prepared for competition showed up for the 1957 Daytona Speed Week. Built by Frank Coons and James Travers, they bore only a superficial resemblance to stock Thunderbirds. The bodies of both cars were completely gutted, aerodynamic panels including an aluminum tonneau for the passenger region were fitted and the stock instrumentation was replaced by a cluster of dials appropriate for a competition sports car. A quick but complete perusal of these "Big Birds" revealed that they possessed the three pri-

**1971 Thunderbird**

**1972 Thunderbird**

mary prerequisites for success in competition: light weight, excellent handling, and plenty of power. The first of these was partially achieved by using many body braces and stiffeners that had been drilled to resemble a metallic version of Swiss cheese. While not terribly sophisticated, the Thunderbird's suspension was brutally efficient. At the front, a splined torsion bar was attached to the lower A-member suspension pieces and coil springs far stiffer than stock were installed. At the rear, Halibrand axles were used and the semi-elliptic springs had additional leaves installed. Heavy-duty tubular shocks were also used. Brakes were cross-finned drums of 2.5 inch diameter. Those at the rear carried a touch of Lincoln's Mexican road racing heritage by having a cooling system incorporating heater motors directing air to the backing plates through flexible tubing. Halibrand magnesium knock-off wheels carried Firestone Super Sport tires. Two additional changes involved the relocation of the Thunderbird's 12-volt battery to the right rear fender and the installation of an additional fuel tank in the trunk.

The use of a 312 cid V-8 in one of the Thunderbirds obviously didn't raise any eyebrows, but imagine the reaction of onlookers to the sight of a big 430 cid Lincoln V-8 in its engine bay! Both engines were equipped with Hilborn fuel injection systems, Scintilla ignitions and McCulloch superchargers. In that form, the 312-engined T-Bird appeared on the beach on February 9 and stormed through the measured mile at 153.126 mph. For the standing start one-mile run, the Thunderbird achieved a speed of 93.312 mph. The Lincoln V-8 powered Thunderbird blew up during the flying

**Following pages, 1973 Thunderbird**

1973

mile competition, but did manage a very impressive standing start run through the mile of 98.065 mph without getting out of third gear! Both cars had four-speed Jaguar transmissions.

NASCAR added a series of sports car races at New Smyrna to the Speed Week's schedule in 1957 and these modified Thunderbirds had no difficulty qualifying. Although the T-Bird with the 430 engine had a quick 79.852 mph lap speed to its credit, it didn't race. However, the 312 V-8 engine Thunderbird which qualified at 77.419 mph, finished second behind Carroll Shelby's 4.9 Ferrari.

The transformation of an automobile such as this, that could run in close company with a Ferrari, into a four-seater that was fully two feet longer, four inches wider and an inch higher was nothing less than revolutionary. But from the time the new model was introduced at one minute past midnight on January 1st, 1958 at the Thunderbird Golf Club in Palm Springs, California, the Bigger Bird was a success. However, its roadability was now that of an American sedan and, reported Tom McCahill ("Mechanic's Illustrated," June, 1958), possessed "not even a remote hint of the sports car feel." Yet the Thunderbird's 205.4-inch overall length still made it a trim car by American standards and its 300 hp 352 cid engine enabled zero to 60 mph times around the ten-second mark possible. Furthermore, a four-seater T-Bird was initially judged to be the winner of the first Daytona 500. Although the photo finish between the Thunderbird, an Oldsmobile and a

**1974 Thunderbird**

**1974 Thunderbird**

**1975 Thunderbird**

Chevrolet was later ruled to have been led by Lee Petty's 1959 Oldsmobile, the ability of the Thunderbird to average over 135 mph for 500 miles needed no apologies. Furthermore, it symbolized the performance that, over the years, maintained a link between the original models and the post-1983 models.

Although production of the 37,892 Thunderbirds (all but 2,134 being hardtops) for the 1958 model season has to be regarded as an impressive vindication of Ford's wisdom in switching to the four-passenger concept, it faded before the 67,456 production level for 1959. One of these Thunderbirds was an extra special car since it was the 50,000,000th automobile produced by Ford. Changes in the year-old T-Bird body were extensive, but experienced Bird watchers had no difficulty in pointing out the 1959's horizontal bar format for its front grille and rear taillight backdrop, and the new arrow-shaped side trim spear.

These types of minor revisions of the 1958 format were also apparent from a quick review of the T-Bird's front suspension, whose design consisted of unequal length A-arms, coil springs and ball joints. Many of these components were interchangeable with those of the larger Fords. One major improvement for 1959 concerned the link-type stabilizer bar which was attached to each wheel below the lower A-arms and limited body roll. For 1959 it was of a larger diameter. At the rear, the coil spring, torque arm and trailing link arrangement of 1958, which did little for the Thunderbird's handling, was replaced by a semi-elliptic leaf spring arrangement that was generally regarded as a substantial improvement.

The base engine for the T-Bird remained the 352 cid V-8, which, in spite of a reduction in compression ratio from 10.2:1 to 9.6:1, still was credited with 300 hp at 4000 rpm and 395 lb-ft of torque at 2800 rpm. An interesting first year option at $177 was the big 430 cid Lincoln V-8 with 340 hp at 4400 rpm and 490 lb-ft of torque at 2800. A compression ratio of 10.0:1 was stated for this engine. Although it was available only with automomatic transmission, this V-8, then the largest in American production, made the T-Bird a potent accelerator. The Thunderbird's road weight now exceeded two tons, but even with a 2.91:1 rear axle ratio, the 430 cid engined models could accelerate from zero to 60 mph in nine seconds and complete the standing start quarter-mile in 17 seconds with a speed of 86.57 mph. An interesting after-market option, offered by Bill Stroppe, was a triple two-barrel setup with an aluminum intake manifold. This raised peak horsepower to approximately 400.

The second generation of four-seater Birds, built from 1961 through 1963, were available with standard 390 cid engines with 300 hp at 4600 rpm and 427 lb-ft of torque available at 2800 rpm. Among the suspension changes for 1961 was what Ford described as "controlled wheel recession," which involved the use of front and rear suspension components allowing a slight amount of fore and aft wheel movement. A by-product of this design at the rear was less spring windup. Also proving beneficial to the Thunderbird's handling was a wider front and rear tread (increased respectively by one and three inches), and re-engineered steering.

Reflecting both the Thunderbird's ever-growing popularity (over 73,000 were produced in 1961) and its favorable public image was "Car and Driver's" August, 1962, summation of its status: "The Thunderbird is firmly entrenched as the standard for other manufacturers to emulate if they want to build 'GT' or 'sporty' cars that the public will buy in any great numbers." Adding further brightness to what was a very strong public image was the new Sports Roadster for 1962. As the most expensive ($5,439) T-Bird it obviously had to be impressive. With a removable fiberglass tonneau cover for the rear seats, it was an outrageously opulent automobile that just about everyone loved. Also standard on this "two-seater" were Kelsey-Hayes chrome wire wheels that were a $373.30 option for other Thunderbirds. During the 1962 model year, a "Sports V-8" option listing for $242 was offered. With three Holley two-barrel carburetors and a 10.5:1 compression ratio, it produced 340 hp at 5000 rpm. Torque was unchanged at 427 lb-ft but was now available at 3600 rpm.

But just two years later, in 1964, when the Thunderbird debuted with its fourth major body style, there was little to connect the T-Bird with exciting performance. The only engine was the 390 cid 300 hp V-8 which provided adequate but hardly startling zero to 60 mph times of 11 + seconds. As "Motor Trend" (February, 1964) observed: "What little performance image T-Birds once had is gone and forgotten. The Bird no longer thunders."

However, this harsh assessment wasn't 100 percent on target. True, the Thunderbird wasn't a supercar, but it wasn't a slug either. The big 428 cid 345 hp engine became an option in 1966 that could push the nearly 5,700 pounds from zero to 60 mph in under 10 seconds. A year earlier, the same front vented disc brakes used by the Lincoln Continental had been introduced on the Thunderbird, giving it a highly respectable deceleration capability. For example, testing a 1969 model, "Car Life" (February, 1969) reported its braking ability from 80 to 0 mph was "higher than all but a handful of cars sold in the U.S."

By the early seventies, all American automobiles were in full retreat from the performance levels of the sixties and neither the Thunderbird's standard 193 hp 429 cid V-8 or the optional 211 hp 460 cid V-8 were high output enough. The only performance options consisted of a 3.25:1 rear axle, Traction-Lok differential and a heavy duty suspension system. Certainly worthy of praise was the four-wheel disc brake option priced at $184.00 in 1975.

But, by 1982, these developments seemed far less important as the Thunderbird, radically reformed by significant size reductions in 1977 and 1982, was on the verge of the most dramatic change in its history. A new era of Thunderbird performance was unfolding, but with the emphasis once again placed on providing the driver with a highly responsive automobile, it was really a case of Ford "coming home."

**1976 Thunderbird**

**1977 Thunderbird**

1977 Thunderbird

1978 Thunderbird

1979 Thunderbird

1979 Thunderbird

1980 Thunderbird

1980 Thunderbird

Following pages, 1955 and 1980 Thunderbirds

# Birds in the Hand: Thunderbird, 1983-1985.

A fundamental new way of designing cars at Ford Motor Company produced dramatically-styled and more fuel-efficient Thunderbirds shaped to slice the air.

"We've learned that aerodynamic car design is a reliable, low-cost way to substantially improve fuel economy as well as create very distinctive products," said Jack J. Telnack, chief design executive, North American Design, at the introduction of the 1983 models.

"A car's engine must overpower resistance the vehicle encounters on the road. The less horsepower required, the better the vehicle's fuel economy." With its sloping hood, concealed drip moldings, tapered front and rear fenders and sharply raked windshield, the 1983 Thunderbird became the most aerodynamic car in its class.

"More than 850 changes were made to the initial Thunderbird design during the hours it spent in the wind tunnel to help improve its aerodynamics," Telnack added. "As a result, the new Thunderbird has a .35 coefficient of drag (CD); a remarkable 17 percent improvement over the 1982 model."

Another way of measuring the aerodynamic efficiency of a vehicle is "aerodynamic" horsepower—the amount of horsepower required to overcome air drag. Studies by Ford experts have shown that in city driving, air resistance consumes about 20 percent of the total horsepower required to move a car. On the highway, however, it accounts for approximately 48 percent of the needed horsepower. The 1983 Thunderbird required only 6.2 hp to overcome air drag at 50 mph.

"We've been able to improve the average drag coefficient of our vehicles considerably in recent years," Tel-

**1983 Thunderbird**

1983 Thunderbird wind tunnel testing

nack pointed out, "going from .51 in 1977 to .40 in 1983."

He added that the 22 percent improvement in average drag coefficient from 1977 to 1983 resulted in an actual improvement in corporate average fuel economy of over one mpg.

"And we've really only begun to utilize the potential of aerodynamics," Telnack said. "We're learning new things about it every day. In the future, we'll be seeing some CD numbers for production cars that would have been considered impossible to reach a few years ago.

"Ford has assumed a leadership role in the application of aerodynamic principals, and we are committing our worldwide resources to maintaining that leadership. After all, there are tremendous consumer benefits resulting from improved aerodynamics.

"In addition to better gas mileage, aerodynamics contributes to improved vehicle stability, better interior ventilation, efficient engine cooling, reduced wind noise and even greater safety through its effectiveness in controlling deposits of dirt, spray or rain on windows.

The 1984 aerodynamic Thunderbird design reflected Ford Motor Company's continued committment to provide the consumer with a highly-styled, performance-oriented car.

The Thunderbird buyer apparently liked what he saw, as T-Bird sales for the 1984 model year were 156,583 units, an increase of 58 percent over 1983 and up 227 percent over 1982. In car-conscious California, Thunderbird was the number one selling nameplate during the 1984 model run.

"The sleek Thunderbird design is a symbol of Ford's new direction for the Eighties—aerodynamic, high tech and ahead of the pack," said Louis E. Lataif, Ford vice-president and Ford Division general manager at the 1984 announcement. "We are continuing to improve and refine an American car classic which was born 30 years ago."

Ford designer William P. Boyer recalled the early history of the car and its development through the years. Mr. Boyer was lead stylist on the original 1955 two-seater Thunderbird and had a hand in designing the 1984s.

"The original Thunderbird was a spontaneous reaction to a national urge for fun motoring," Mr. Boyer said. "As a premier American sporty car, Thunderbird inspired many imitators and created a niche for fun-driving sporty cars on the American automotive scene.

"From the very beginning, Thunderbird captured the enthusiasm of its many followers by setting trends. A removable hardtop, power windows, and seat belts were part of the magic of the first 'Bird. Today, the magic is dramatic aerodynamic styling that holds the car to the road and lets it whisper through the wind."

For Mr. Boyer, nearing the end of his 33-year career as a Ford designer, his Thunderbird years have not been without controversy. "When you are trying to design a car to be ahead of its time, sometimes you're right on and other times you are not so right. I think we were more often on target with Thunderbird than not, having produced and sold more than 2.65 million of them in 30 years."

The first Thunderbird rolled off the line at Ford's Dearborn, Michigan Assembly Plant on September 9, 1954, with public introduction on November 12. Although only 54,000 Thunderbirds were purchased in its first three years, the early T-Birds quickly became favorites for car collectors everywhere.

The 1985 Thunderbird has a crisper look, fore and aft, as well as an all-new instrument panel. Additionally, there is more power for the Turbo Coupe and a host of new comfort, convenience and performance options. The appearance improvements include a new color-keyed grille, new full-width taillamps—with inboard backup lamps—and a new Thunderbird emblem.

Major interior improvements include a new instrument panel and a new split-bench reclining seat in cloth trim, with a consolette featuring a folding armrest and a coin holder. Door trim panels with assist straps, storage bins, and carpeting on the lower portion are also new. A third seat belt in the rear allows five-passenger seating.

The all-new instrument panel configuration is clearly driver-oriented with a contemporary electronic LCD speedometer and combination odometer/trip odometer. Added to the optional all-electronic instrument cluster is a high-tech electronic tachometer with a graphic readout and overlayed electronic ammeter, oil, temperature and fuel gauges. Fuel levels may be displayed digitally, with a flashing feature to indicate low fuel.

The Thunderbird Turbo Coupe instrument panel features a performance cluster with analog speedometer, tachometer, turbo boost, fuel, temperature, ammeter and oil pressure gauges—all located directly in front of the driver. Other interior refinements include an easy-grip, soft-feel sport steering wheel developed especially for the performance driving requirements of the Turbo Coupe.

Elan, Turbo Coupe and FILA models have new four-way adjustable head restraints on the front seats. Base model and Elan split-bench seats are separated by the consolette and fold-down armrests. The articulated sport seat for Turbo Coupe and FILA models has a power lumbar support adjustment, replacing the squeeze-bulb system on previous systems.

Engine refinements further improve Thunderbird's performance image. Most significant is a modified 2.3-liter Turbo Coupe engine with full electronic boost control and higher flow-rate fuel injectors to deliver even more power than last year's turbo.

To use this added power more efficiently, there is a five-speed manual overdrive transmission with new gear ratios and an improved shifter with shorter throws than last year's transmission. That means quicker, smoother gear changes.

Turbo Coupe power steering effort for new models is increased, providing better road feel, and unidirectional "Gatorback" performance tires on unique 15x7-inch aluminum wheels enhance the car's traction and road manners.

New options include power seat recliners, heated front seats, alloy wheels, a new graphic equalizer, upgraded cassette players, and an all-new Electronic Climate Control air-conditioner incorporating an advanced all-electronic pushbutton control panel.

Also in 1985, Ford Thunderbird, an American highway legend, celebrates its 30th anniversary with a special, limited edition model. U.S. production of the

**1985 Thunderbird interior**

special models, which begins in mid-1985, will be limited to 5,000 units.

Based on the top-of-the-line Thunderbird Elan model, the commemorative Thunderbird features medium regatta blue clearcoat metallic paint and unique bodyside molding and tape treatment.

Buyers of the 30th Anniversary car receive an array of special commemorative items including special instrument panel and decklid badges; ignition keys with profiles of the 1955 and 1985 models; a matching blue key chain with the Thunderbird logo; floor mats with the anniversary logo; an owner's manual holder with a Thunderbird history booklet; and a leather jacket, designed by Members Only, with the Thunderbird emblem.

Ford's quick-off-the-mark 5.0-liter V-8 engine, Automatic Overdrive (AOD) transmission, P225 performance tires, 15x7 cast aluminum wheels, and handling suspension are standard. Also standard are an electronic instrument cluster, electronic AM/FM stereo search radio with cassette tape player, graphic equalizer, electronic climate control, speed control, power door locks, tilt leather-wrapped steering wheel, rear window defroster, and power antenna. Dual driver and passenger six-way power seats are features on the split-bench seating with a unique regatta blue cloth trim.

Exterior features include bodycolor grille, headlamp doors, mirror bodies, lower moldings, black greenhouse moldings, "B" pillar and taillamp appliques, door handles, black chrome door and decklid lock bezels and a dark charcoal radio antenna base.

**Following pages, 1955 and 1985 Thunderbirds**

# Flatfoot Musclecars: Ford Police Cruisers.

All the high performance cars weren't sold to the general public. Some of the hottest went to law enforcement authorities. In fact, many of the early high performance options in Detroit were civilian versions of the police packages being offered by Ford, Chevy, Olds and so on. Sometimes these were detuned a bit for civilian use; sometimes not. Eventually, there was an odd turn about, with many police departments (especially in metropolitan areas) becoming more interested in economy. As a consequence, many police options took a turn toward tameness just when the civilian high performance rigs were reaching their fire-breathing heights. Nevertheless, the police packages form an intriguing part of the Ford high performance story and a sampling of them appears on the following pages, drawn from the Ford police brochures.

## '63 FORD POLICE INTERCEPTOR

*sets a new standard for high performance and durability*

The extra measure of performance engineered into the '63 Police Interceptor makes it the finest maximum-duty police vehicle available. Powered by Ford's famous Police Interceptor 4-V/390 V-8 engine, it puts you in command of *any* situation.

The Ford Interceptor engine, made exclusively for law enforcement agencies, is specially built for absolute peak performance at sustained high speeds. Combined with Synchro-Smooth Drive—America's first fully synchronized 3-speed manual transmission—or floor-shift 4-speed all-synchronized manual, or the new Interceptor Cruise-O-Matic transmission—a recommended option—the Interceptor 4-V/390 V-8 provides extremely fast acceleration.

For greater stability and handling properties, the Police Interceptor is equipped with a rugged, heavy-duty suspension system, including heavy-duty springs and shock absorbers. These, along with the heavy-duty stabilizer bar included in the Hi-Speed and Handling Package, provide sure stability and precision control through any pursuit-speed maneuvering. Large, heavy-duty brakes are fitted with specially molded linings and groove-cooled drums to resist brake fading in "hot" stops.

Cruising comfort and roominess are other driver benefits in the Police Interceptor. Ford's new heavy-duty, full-width front seat—angled at the ideal posture position—combines maximum head room with firm spring support and thick padding in the cushion and back for greater comfort and durability.

Ford Police Interceptor has the expanded 1963 Ford service-saving features that reduce maintenance costs more than ever, as a result of the greater durability of this quality-built Ford vehicle. The Police Interceptor is available as a complete package, in 2-door and 4-door Ford 300 and Galaxie Series, with the equipment listed below.

### EQUIPMENT INCLUDED IN POLICE INTERCEPTOR PACKAGE:

- 330-hp Police Interceptor 4-V/390 V-8
- Extra-Cooling Radiator
- 70 Amp-hr HD Battery
- Manual 3-Speed Fully Synchronized Transmission
- 11-Inch Clutch
- Hi-Speed and Handling Package, includes HD Springs, HD Extra-Control Shock Absorbers and HD Stabilizer Bar
- HD Fade-Resistant Brakes with Riveted Linings
- Certified Calibration Speedometer (2 mph increments)
- HD Seats with Maximum Head Room, Full-Width Front Seat
- HD Floor Mats, Black Rubber, Front and Rear

### HIGHLY RECOMMENDED OPTIONS

- 15" Tires and Wheels (LPO)
- Interceptor Cruise-O-Matic Transmission (LPO)
- Padded Instrument Panel and Two Cushioned Sun Visors (RPO)
- Front Seat Belts for Driver and Passenger (RPO)

## *There's blazing power in this mighty*

## INTERCEPTOR 4-V/390 V-8

| | |
|---|---|
| Displacement | 390 cu. in. |
| Horsepower @ rpm | 330 @ 5000 |
| Torque (lbs-ft) @ rpm | 427 @ 3200 |
| Compression Ratio | 10.5 to 1 |
| Carburetor | 4-venturi |
| Fuel | premium |
| Transmission-Axle Ratios: | |
| 3- or 4-Speed Manual or Overdrive | 3.50 to 1 |
| | (opt.) 3.89 to 1 |
| Interceptor Cruise-O-Matic | 3.00 to 1 |

### '63 FORD POLICE CRUISER

For high power, but less demanding performance peaks than required with the Police Interceptor, the rugged Police Cruiser is recommended. Identical to the Interceptor in everything but power, the Police Cruiser has a 300-hp Thunderbird 4-V/390 V-8 engine. Package equipment and recommended options are the same, except for the engine and regular Cruise-O-Matic Drive.

**THUNDERBIRD 4-V/390 V-8**

| | |
|---|---|
| Displacement | 390 cu. in. |
| Horsepower @ rpm | 300 @ 4600 |
| Torque (lbs-ft) @ rpm | 427 @ 2800 |
| Compression Ratio | 10.5 to 1 |
| Carburetor | 4-venturi |
| Fuel | premium |
| Transmission-Axle Ratios: | |
| 3- or 4-Speed Manual or Overdrive | 3.50 to 1 |
| | (opt.) 3.89 to 1 |
| Cruise-O-Matic | 3.00 to 1 |

The Interceptor 4-V/390 V-8 is a specially engineered 330-hp powerplant designed *exclusively for* and sold only to law enforcement agencies. Its terrific acceleration and high-sustained power are the result of a carefully "souped up" induction system, including special high-lift camshaft, solid valve tappets, high-performance valve springs with solid retainers and internal damping springs to provide reliable valve operation at high speeds. The freer-breathing Super-Filter air cleaner and high-velocity 4-venturi carburetor enable peak performance. Exhaust valves are forged of special alloy and exhaust manifolds are low-restriction header type, plus low back-pressure mufflers for maximum power.

Along with these special features, the new Interceptor engine has all of Ford's advanced-design and service-saving features: deep-block construction; short-stroke design with super-fitted alloy pistons and efficient, wedge-type combustion chambers; heavy-duty copper-lead main and connecting rod bearings; 6,000-mile Full-Flow oil filter; 30,000-mile dry-type air cleaner; 36,000-mile fuel filter; and 36,000-mile or two-year coolant-antifreeze (available—factory installed).

## *Other Options Available for* INTERCEPTOR *and* CRUISER

### RPO—MONTHLY SCHEDULE ITEMS

*Electric Windshield Washer
2-Speed Electric Windshield Wipers
*AM Radio (full-transistor)—Push Button
*AM/FM Radio (full-transistor)—Push Button
Tinted Glass (windshield only or all around)
*Backup Lights
4-Speed Fully Synchronized Transmission, Floor-Mounted Shift
Overdrive Transmission
Optional Axle Ratios (see specifications)
*Swift Sure Power Brakes
*Master-Guide Power Steering
Power Front Seat
Power-Lift Door Windows
*Remote Control Outside Rearview Mirror (left side)
*Deluxe Outside Rearview Mirror (left or right side)
Deletion of MagicAire Heater †

*†Heater is installed during production unless otherwise specified. If deleted, an appropriate price reduction is made.*

### LPO—LIMITED PRODUCTION ITEMS

Beige, Green or Red All-Vinyl Upholstery and Trim
Rear Arm Rests (Ford 300)
Ash Receptacle in Front Seat Back (Ford 300 4-dr. model)
*Inside Non-Glare Mirror
Outside-Mounted Door Mirror (left or right side)
Padded Instrument Panel
Extra-Cooling Viscous Drive 1.25 Ratio Fan (smaller water-pump ratio, slip disc fan slips at 1,600 rpm)
Radio Noise Suppression Equipment
Generator Option—40-Amp. HD Low Cut-In
Alternator Option—40-Amp. or 60-Amp. HD Pancake Type with Built-In Silicon Rectifier
Five 6.70 x 15 or 7.10 x 15 or 8.00 x 14 4 or 6 pr. Tubeless or Tube-Type Tires; also Whitewall Tires
Winter Tread Rear Tires
Extra-Heavy-Duty Seats (front head room slightly less than package seat)

### DSO—SPECIAL ORDER ITEMS

Generator Options—40-Amp. Standard Type; HD 50-Amp. Low Cut-In or 60-Amp.
Alternator Options—60-Amp. HD Std. or EHD Types or 100-Amp. EHD with Built-In Silicon Rectifier
Charge Indicator Gauge
Oil Pressure Gauge
1¾" I.D. Conduit for Radio Cable
Radio Mounting Base in Luggage Compartment for Radio Equipment
Spare Tire Relocation (to accommodate radio equipment)
Suppression Spark Plugs with Non-Suppressed Ignition Wiring
Simultaneous Flashing Parking and Taillights
Simultaneous Flashing Red Grille Lights and Taillights
Spotlamp—Cowl Mount without Mirror (specify red flashing or clear sealed beam)
Spotlamp—Door Mount with Mirror (specify red flashing or clear sealed beam)
Pace-Type Speedometer with Special Needle Stop
Special Map Light (auxiliary lamp under instrument panel)
*Front Seat Belts—Driver or Passenger
Hand Throttle, Locking Type
Single-Key Locking System (one key for all locks in car or fleet)
Electric Window Regulators for Front Windows only
Ceramic Fuel Filters

### DEALER INSTALLED ITEMS

Parking Brake Warning Light
Body Mount Rearview Mirrors
Bumper Guards, Front and/or Rear
Deluxe Rear Antenna
Fire Extinguishers
Plus many other customary accessories

**Also dealer installed*

### EXPLANATION OF TERMS

**RPO**
Regular Production Option. Equipment advertised nationally and available without delay in production.
**LPO**
Limited Production Option. Equipment generally used only by fleet and commercial accounts. Slight delays possible.
**DSO**
Domestic Special Order. Specific procurement, with time necessary to fill order.

# LOWEST FIRST COST... LOWEST UPKEEP...

Fairlane's low price tag, genuine reputation for quality and designed-in service-saving features make it the ideal police vehicle where low first cost and minimal upkeep are the watchwords. With big car features, the Fairlane is a big performer, as well. The Trooper Package for Fairlane Police Cars is built around a 390-cu. in. powerplant that delivers 320 horsepower worth of power-packed performance. Three other engines, including an economy-minded 200-cu. in. Six, round out the selection of Fairlane police performance options. Fairlane Police Cars are available in 2-door and 4-door models with options available to fit the needs and budget of any law enforcement agency.

FAIRLANE 500 2-DOOR SEDAN
*Also available in 4-Door Sedan*

## FAIRLANE "POLICE SPECIAL" PACKAGES

Fairlane 2-door and 4-door sedans can be equipped with any of these four special police car packages.

### *TROOPER*

A powerful 390-cu. in., 4-barrel V-8 engine gives Fairlane plenty of power and speed for pursuit or sustained highway patrol work. This 320-hp engine is designed and built for smooth, dependable and efficient performance all day long at normal road patrol speeds.

The Trooper Package includes: 42-Amp. Alternator with Single Belt Drive □ Heavy-Duty Battery—70 Amp. □ Heavy-Duty Front Springs, Rear Springs and Shock Absorbers □ Heavy-Duty Black Rubber Floor Mats, Front and Rear □ Extra Cooling Package □ Calibrated Speedometer with 2-Mile-Per-Hour Increments □ Heavy-Duty Front Seat with Foam Padding.

### *PACER*

This popular package features a 390-cu. in., 2-barrel V-8. This snappy 270-hp engine delivers fast acceleration and high speeds second only to the Trooper engine. All other special features are identical to those in the Trooper Package.

### *RANGER*

Powered by a 289-cu. in., 200-hp V-8, the Ranger Package gives the Fairlane police car good power and speed with unusually thrifty operation. With the exception of the engine, the Ranger has all the special features listed under the Trooper.

### *SENTRY*

This package is built around the thrifty 200-cu. in., 120-hp Six. It's a fine performer in city traffic patrol work where economy and dependability are most important. 3-speed fully synchronized transmission with heavy-duty clutch is standard. All other package features are shared with the Trooper, with the addition of the wear-resistant brake option.

# FAIRLANE POLICE CARS

FAIRLANE 4-DOOR SEDAN
*Also available in 2-Door Sedan*

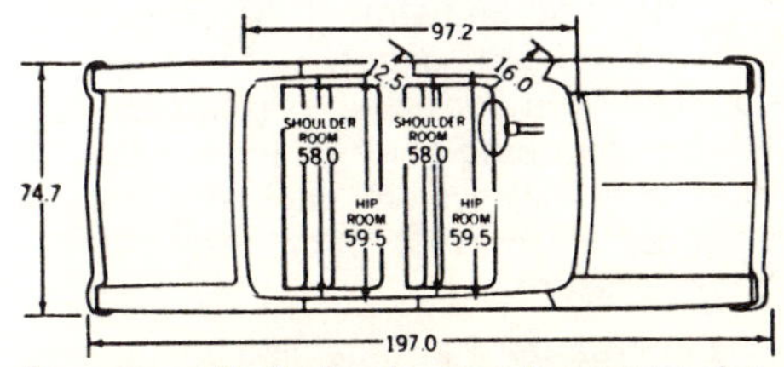

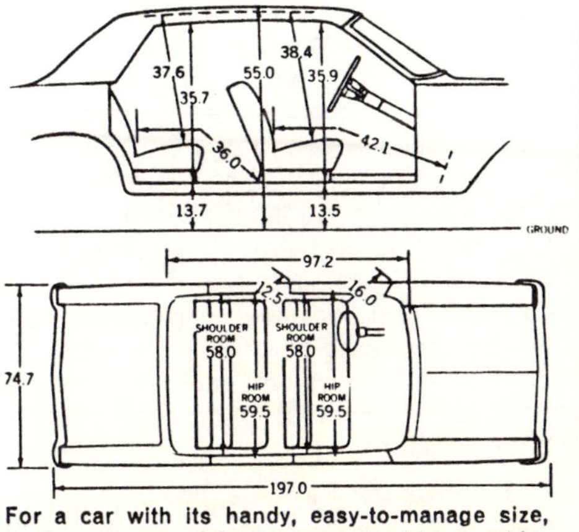

For a car with its handy, easy-to-manage size, Fairlane is surprisingly roomy inside, provides easy access, dutifully large trunk space.

## FAIRLANE POLICE CAR POWER TEAM SELECTIONS

| PACKAGE | TROOPER | PACER | RANGER | SENTRY |
|---|---|---|---|---|
| ENGINES | Thunderbird Spec. V-8 | Thunderbird V-8 | Challenger V-8 | Fairlane Six |
| Displacement (cu. in.) | 390 4V | 390 2V | 289 2V | 200 1V |
| Horsepower @ rpm | 320 @ 4800 | 270 @ 4400 | 200 @ 4400 | 120 @ 4400 |
| Torque (lbs-ft) @ rpm | 427 @ 3200 | 403 @ 2600 | 282 @ 2400 | 190 @ 2400 |
| Compression Ratio (to 1) | 10.5 | 9.5 | 9.3 | 9.2 |
| Alternator | 42 amp. (single) | 42 amp. (single) | 42 amp. (single) | 42 amp. (single) |
| Transmission | 3-speed man. | 3-speed man. | 3-speed man. | 3-speed man. |
| Clutch (dia. in.) | 11.5 | 11 | 10.0 | 9.4 |
| Battery (amp-hr) | 70 HD | 70 HD | 70 HD | 70 HD |
| AXLE RATIOS | | | | |
| 3-Speed Manual | 3.00 (3.25)/3.00/ | 3.00 (3.25)/3.00/ | 2.79† (3.25)/3.00/3.25† | 3.25 (3.50)†/3.25/3.25† 3.25* |
| 4-Speed Manual (opt.) | 3.00 (3.25)/3.25/ | 3.00 (3.25)/3.25/ | 3.25 (3.00)†/3.25/3.25† | N.A. |
| Overdrive (opt.) | N.A. | N.A. | 3.50 | N.A. |
| Cruise-O-Matic (opt.) | 3.00 (3.25)/3.00/ | 3.00 (3.25)/3.00/ | 2.79† (3.00)†/3.00/3.00† | 2.79† (3.25)/3.25/3.25† 3.25* |

Axles per ratios listed here are available with self-adjusting brakes only except where noted. Optional ratio shown in parenthesis. Limited-slip differential axle ratio shown in brackets. 3.00, 3.25 limited-slip differential axle ratios available optionally with 200 and 289 engines have heavy-duty brakes as standard. *Optional axle ratio with wear-resistant (bonded), manually adjusted brakes. †Optional axle ratio with heavy-duty (riveted) manually adjusted brakes.

# America's leader in Police Cars

More law enforcement agencies from coast to coast buy Ford than any other product to make it *the number one police car* in America.

In '68, there is a choice of five power packages in 2- and 4-door sedans and station wagons. They range from the thrifty, dependable 6-cylinder, 150-hp Deputy to the maximum performance 360-hp Interceptor.

New '68 features mean even greater value. They include more efficient floating-caliper power front disc brakes. They're standard on the Interceptor, optional on all others. Heavy-duty, fade-resistant drum-type brakes, front and rear, with manual adjusters, are standard on Guardian, Cruiser, Deputy and Sentinel. Self-adjusters are optional.

In addition, every Ford police car has been designed with heavier duty components, to help insure maximum durability for rugged police work. Some of these "police special" items include heavy-duty front seat springs and padding, for solid comfort and extended wear. And there's Ford's police maximum handling package, standard on police cars. It has heavy-duty front and rear springs, extra control shocks and a heavy-duty front stabilizer bar. Other features include: calibrated speedometer with 2-mph increments, heavy-duty front and rear black rubber floor mats, extra cooling package and 6-inch wheel rims with nylon tires.

It all adds up to dependable service and value, making Ford the number one choice with police departments across America.

### POLICE CAR SERIES AND MODELS

**FORD:** Custom 500, 2-Door and 4-Door; Custom, 2-Door and 4-Door; Wagons: Country Sedan, Custom 500 Ranch Wagon, Ranch Wagon

**FAIRLANE:** Fairlane 4-Door Sedan, 2-Door Hardtop

**ECONOLINE VAN:** Ambulance Conversion, Personnel Carrier

**BRONCO:** Pickup, Wagon, Roadster

# FORD...THE POLICE CARS THA

## FORD "POLICE SPECIAL" PACKAGES

The following five "Police Special" packages, available only to law enforcement agencies, have been individually tailored to meet the performance specification of local requirements. These packages are available with any Ford Police Car and have been developed with heavier duty components for greater reliability, to stand up to the demands of rugged police work.

### INTERCEPTOR

This package is powered by a husky 428-cu. in. V-8 engine with a 4-barrel carburetor. The engine develops 360 hp and 459 lbs-ft torque, and is built to provide very fast takeoffs and sustained high speed driving in day-to-day patrol work. Speeds in excess of 120 mph are well within the range of this powerplant. The Ford designed and built 4-barrel carburetor offers smooth, steady idle characteristics, better starting when the engine is warm, automatic positive acting choke, and fewer service adjustments. The valve train features a high-lift camshaft, hydraulic lifters for automatic adjustment, precision-fitted exhaust valves, high performance valve springs with one-piece retainers and internal damping springs. In addition, the dual exhaust system (not available in wagons) is a low restriction design for less back pressure.

The Interceptor Package also includes the following items:

80-Amp. Heavy-Duty Battery □ 42-Amp.

# DELIVER PERFORMANCE AND RELIABILITY

FORD CUSTOM 4-DOOR

Alternator with Dual Belt Drive □ Power Front Disc Brakes with Self-Adjusting Heavy-Duty Fade-Resistant Drum-Type Rear Brakes □ Police Maximum Handling Package with Extra-Heavy-Duty Front and Rear Springs, Extra Control Shock Absorbers and Heavy-Duty Front Stabilizer Bar □ Calibrated Speedometer with 2-Mile-Per-Hour Increments □ Extra Cooling Package □ Lubricator-Fitted Driveshaft □ Heavy-Duty Front Seat Springs and Padding □ Heavy-Duty Front and Rear Vinyl-Coated Black Rubber Floor Mats □ 6-Inch Wheel Rims with Nylon Tires.

### CRUISER

A high performance 390-cu. in. V-8 engine with a 4-barrel carburetor powers this package. The engine develops 315 hp and 427 lbs-ft torque. The Cruiser shares all other Special Police features with the Interceptor with these exceptions: 70-amp. battery, single belt drive alternator, heavy-duty clutch, heavy-duty fade-resistant drum-type brakes with manual adjusters front and rear, heavy-duty steering column (with manual transmission).

### GUARDIAN

The Guardian Package is built around a 390-cu. in., 2-barrel carburetor V-8 engine. It develops 265 hp and 390 lbs-ft torque. The engine is designed to use regular fuel, and combines good operating economy along with dependable around-the-clock performance. Aside from the single exhaust system, the outstanding features of the Guardian Package are the same as listed under the Cruiser.

### SENTINEL

The Sentinel Package provides a good combination of smooth V-8 power and a measure of economy. The heart of the package is Ford's new 302-cu. in. 2-barrel carburetor engine which develops 210 hp. and 300 lbs-ft torque. The Sentinel Package shares the same Police Special features listed with the Cruiser and Guardian.

### DEPUTY

Power for the Deputy Package is supplied by a 240-cu. in., 6-cylinder engine. It provides traditional Ford "Six" economy along with dependable, peppy performance. The Deputy develops 150 hp and assures a smooth getaway with its high torque at low rpm—234 @ 2200. It shares with the Cruiser, Guardian and Sentinel all the outstanding Police Special features.

# LTD II Standard Features

***The LTD II "S" and LTD II Series are roomy, six-passenger mid-size cars with a trim, budget price—yet feature an impressive list of standard features.***

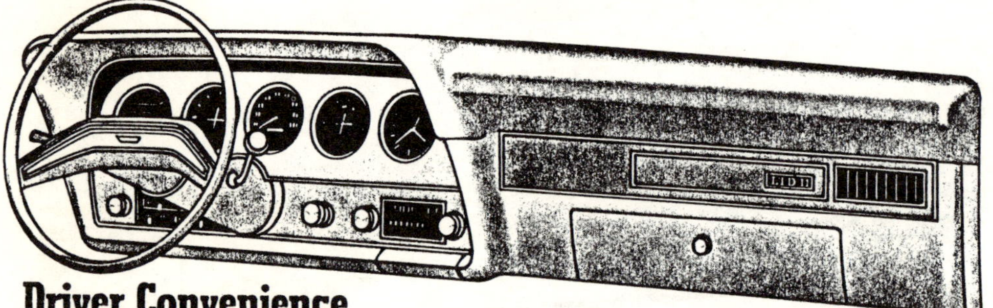

## Driver Convenience

The LTD II instrument panel provides convenience for the driver and ample roominess for front seat passengers. Instruments and controls are arranged directly in front of the driver for easy viewing and reach.

## Automatic Transmission

P R N D 2 1

Ford's versatile automatic transmission provides smooth, even, quiet shifting. The Police Package transmission includes a first gear lock-out feature designed to eliminate the possibility of holding the transmission in first gear. The transmission can be held manually in second gear, and when placed in "Drive" position, the transmission provides fully automatic three-speed operation. (A first gear lock-out delete option is available.)

## Increased Corrosion Protection

Every LTD II is protected against corrosion through the use of precoated steel in fenders, quarter panels, doors, decklids and wheelhousings. Further protection against corrosion is provided through the use of plastic splash shields under the front fenders.

## Seating Comfort

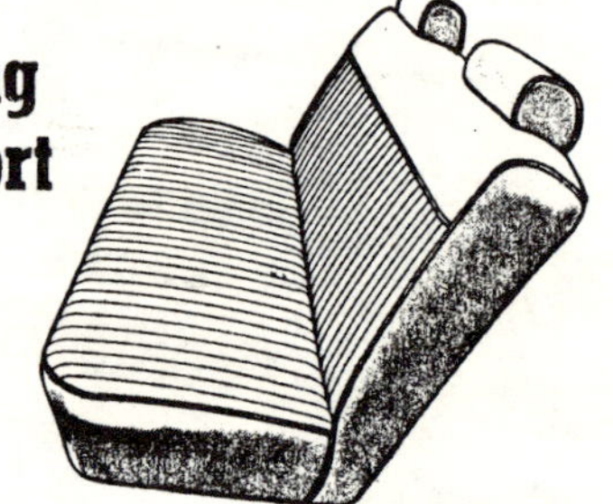

Ford's wide heavy-duty bench seats provide all-day comfort for the driver and plenty of stretch-out room for passengers. The seats include heavy-duty springs and thick molded seat pads. Comfortable cloth covered seats with easy-to-clean vinyl trim are standard. On LTD II series models, the standard front seat is a flight bench design with fold-down armrest; a bench seat option with price credit also is available. Both the flight bench and bench can be ordered with optional all-vinyl trim.

## Solid State Ignition

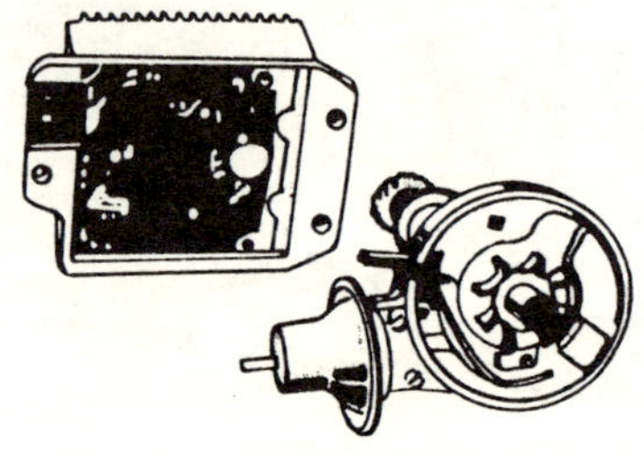

DuraSpark solid-state ignition offers significant advantages over the conventional ignition system by eliminating breaker points and condenser, and providing a stronger spark. The elimination of points and condenser also eliminates a major cause of ignition problems. Less periodic maintenance is required and spark plug life is increased.

## Coolant Recovery System

The 1977 LTD II is equipped with a standard coolant recovery system to preserve the coolant and guard against overheating. The system provides for collecting and recycling any coolant overflow back into the cooling system.

## *Plus These Additional Standard Features:*

- ☐ ***Dual Vertically Stacked Rectangular Headlamps***
- ☐ ***Padded All-Vinyl Door Trim Panels***
- ☐ ***Color-Keyed Instrument Panel with Five Pod Instrument Cluster***
- ☐ ***Cigarette Lighter***
- ☐ ***Lockable Glove Box***
- ☐ ***DirectAire Ventilation***
- ☐ ***3-Speed Heater-Defroster***
- ☐ ***26-gallon Fuel Tank***
- ☐ ***Inside Hood Release***

In addition to these standard features on Ford LTD II Police cars, many options are available so that individual units can be tailored to meet specialized requirements.

# LTD II

## The All-New Mid-Size Pursuit Car

Ford's new 1977 LTD II offers the traditional high level of craftsmanship of the full-size LTD in a comfortable mid-size car that's trimmer in size *and* price. Big on the inside for plenty of passenger room, LTD II is trim on the outside for easy, fast maneuverability.

The LTD II "S" and the LTD II 2-door hardtops and 4-door Pillared Hardtop models are ideally suited to all-around patrol assignments, including pursuit duty. Two Police Packages are available on the four LTD II models. The *351 Police Package* is capable of performing a variety of police assignments and features the 351 CID V-8 engine for brisk performance, economical operation and outstanding durability.

The *400 Police Package* features the popular 400 CID V-8 engine and fills the requirements for general patrol duty, with emphasis on city and suburban cruising. The 400 CID engine also features Ford's DuraSpark solid-state ignition.

An automatic transmission with first gear lock-out, power steering and power brakes (front disc/rear drum) are standard with all LTD II Police Packages.

### LTD II Police Packages

The following equipment is included in the 351 and 400 Police Packages:

- ☐ ***Automatic Transmission with First Gear Lock-Out***
- ☐ ***Heavy-Duty 9" Traction-Lok, Four-Pinion Rear Axle***
- ☐ ***3.00:1 Rear Axle Ratio (2.75:1 in California)***
- ☐ ***Single Exhaust System***
- ☐ ***Power Front Disc/Rear 11-inch Flared Drum Brakes with Organic Linings***
- ☐ ***Heavy-Duty Frame***
- ☐ ***Heavy-Duty Handling Suspension with Rear Stabilizer Bar***
- ☐ ***70-Ampere Alternator***
- ☐ ***Heavy-Duty 77-Ampere-Hour Battery***
- ☐ ***Cloth and Vinyl Interior***
- ☐ ***Heavy-Duty Front Seat***
- ☐ ***0-140 mph Speedometer calibrated in 2 mph Increments***
- ☐ ***Heavy-Duty 15-inch Wheels with 6.5-inch Safety Rims***
- ☐ ***Maximum Cooling Package***
- ☐ ***Transistorized Voltage Regulator***
- ☐ ***HR70 x 15 BSW "Police Special" Tires***
- ☐ ***Power Steering with Front Mounted Oil Cooler***
- ☐ ***Remote Control Decklid Release***
- ☐ ***Transmission Oil Cooler***

# The Original Ponycar: The Story of the Mustang.

By Robert C. Ackerson

Just two months after its introduction, the Mustang, in June, 1964, thundered into the high performance corral with its 271 hp engine. Ford described this V-8 as intended "for the true driving enthusiast who wants sports car performance to complement Mustang's sports car styling." Lee Iacocca rather modestly observed that "271 hp in a car weighing about 2,500 pounds could offer interesting and sporty transportation combined with the ability to idle along in traffic whenever necessary." To be sure, the 271 hp engine could behave itself in traffic before making a quick getaway (zero to 60 mph in 7.5 seconds) en route to a top speed of 117 mph.

Available only with the 271 hp engine or the 225 hp 289 cid Challenger Special V-8 was the Mustang GT Equipment Group, which consisted of ten components. While some of these features were of the cosmetic variety (GT front fender badges, lower body triple stripes), the bulk of this option's $165.03 price paid for some worthwhile hardware. Higher rate front and rear springs, larger shocks and front stabilizer bar plus 22:1 steering (all of which was offered as a separate "Special Handling Package," priced at $30.64), gave the 271 hp Mustang excellent stability and flat cornering. The early Mustangs hadn't been praised for their great brakes, but the inclusion of front disc brakes in the GT option went a long way toward changing that reputation. Other key features included dual straight-through exhausts with flared, chrome tailpipe extensions, four-inch grille-mounted fog lamps and a five-dial (fuel, temperature, speedometer, oil pressure and amperes) instrument cluster. To round out the sporting character of a 271 hp Mustang with the GT Group, a $69.30 Rally Pac, consisting of clock, tachometer, racing mirrors, styled steel wheels plus either red band or white sidewall tires, was also available.

If even more power than that supplied by the 271 hp engine was desired, Ford was happy to provide a number of Cobra-derived options for a customer wanting to own an "ultra-Mustang." For $245, a Cobra dual four-barrel induction kit was offered. In addition to the twin carburetors, special air cleaners and a cast aluminum intake manifold were provided. The total package, explained Ford, "helps develop maximum speed and horsepower in engines modified for hot competition." If "high rpm action" was desired, then the $49.80 Cobra distributor kit was in a Mustang owner's future. It included a heavy-duty distributor and leads, dual points and a centrifugal spark advance. Available for Mustangs with either the 260 cid or 289 cid V-8 was a Cobra cam kit retailing for $75.10. Ford noted that it

**1965 Mustang**

"consists of a finely machined camshaft and 16 tappets of the same type used in winning Cobras."

No significant changes were made in the high performance portion of the Mustang's specifications in 1966 but the following year, Ford offered the 390 cid Thunderbird Special V-8 as a Mustang option for the first time. Priced at a reasonable $158.08, it provided 320 hp at 4800 rpm and 427 lb-ft of torque at 3200 rpm.

The Mustang was redesigned for 1967, but the 390 V-8 added several hundred pounds of weight to the front wheels as compared to a Mustang with the standard six-cylinder engine. To cope with this situation, 390 Mustangs had front springs with a 260 lb/in rate and a 0.72-inch diameter stabilizer bar. In addition, a $388.53 Competition Handling Package was offered with even stiffer springs, Koni adjustable shocks, 16:1 steering, 3.21:1 limited slip differential and front disc brakes. These components could, if so desired, replace the Special Handling Package segment of the GT Equipment Group, which for 1967 was, with a $205.05 price, available with any of four less powerful V-8s, as well as the 271 hp and 320 hp 390 cid V-8s. These latter engines had exhaust systems featuring low-restriction dual mufflers with chromed quad outlets. The 390 engine could propel a Mustang from zero to 60 mph in a little over seven seconds. Yet, it stands out in Mustang performance history as less than an unqualified success due to the exceptional ability of the Chevrolet Camaros with their 350 cid and 396 cid V-8s.

Although the 271 hp engine was dropped for 1968, the Mustang continued to gain stature as a high performance automobile with the availability of two important high-output Ford engines. The first was a 390 hp Cobra 427 V-8. Offered only with Cruise-O-Matic and priced at a hefty $622.97, this engine with hydraulic lifters wasn't a carbon copy of the true Cobra 427 but, with lightweight pistons, super-duty crankcase and connecting rods and a 10.9:1 compression ratio, its credentials were above reproach.

However, the Cobra 427's tenure as a Mustang engine was extremely short, as it was no longer available after December, 1967. Filling the resulting gap quite nicely was the 428 Cobra Jet. Its price was $420.96 above an equivalent Mustang equipped with a 195 hp, 289 cid V-8. Among the 428 Cobra Jet's pertinent standard features was a vacuum-activated Ram Air hood scoop, 735 cfm Holley four-barrel carburetor, healthy-sized intake and exhaust ports, 2900 cam, 10.6:1 compression ratio, plus cylinder heads, valve

**1966 Mustang**

**1967 Mustang**

**1968 Mustang**

springs and dampers seen previously on the 427 engine. The result was a healthy 335 hp at 5400 rpm and 440 lb-ft at 3400 rpm.

Although that multitude of cubic inches made a 428 Mustang somewhat of an incredible hulk in the corners, they also prompted "Hot Rod" (March, 1968) to describe it as "the fastest-running Pure Stock in the history of man." Zero to 60 mph was accomplished in less than six seconds, while the standing start quarter mile was covered in 13.56 seconds with a terminal speed of 106.6 mph.

The 428 Cobra Jet was available with either automatic or four-speed manual transmission. The standard axle carried a 3.50:1 ratio, but either a 3.91 or 4.30 limited slip differential was offered. Goodyear Polyglas F70x14 wide-oval tires were fitted on six-inch rims. On special order, all sound-deadening material could be eliminated if an owner was willing to accept more interior noise as the price for more speed.

A phantom engine that appeared in Ford sales

**1969 Mustang**

literature but seldom, if ever, materialized as a bona fide Mustang option was the 302 cid tunnel port V-8. Late in 1967 this engine was supposedly available on special order, but it's doubtful if any were actually delivered. The following year, Ford formally announced the Tunnel Port with ultra-conservative ratings of 240 hp at 5000 rpm and 310 lb-ft at 3000 rpm. However, in spite of its use in Trans-Am competition, it still was not placed in anything resembling volume production.

Regardless of this will o' the wisp scenario, the 302 numerals were destined to become synonymous with super-performance wrapped up in a Mustang package. Moreover, the high performance 302 engine debuted in 1969, a point in time that has come to be regarded as the age of fulfillment for Ford's street stormers.

The small caliber member of the trio of rapid transit Mustangs for 1969, the Boss 302, was the result of what Ford described as an effort to "build a reasonably quick machine with light power-to-weight ratio." This was an age when superlatives tended to jumble up upon each other whenever American supercars were discussed, but the Boss 302 had little difficulty in living up to the multitude of praise that came its way. Its engine had all the right things in the right places: four-bolt caps on bearings Nos. 2, 3 and 4, inclined valves with 2.25-inch (intake) and 1.71-inch (exhaust) dimensions, an aluminum high-rise manifold sprouting a 780 cfm Holley four-barrel, low restriction headers and a dual-point ignition. Rated at 290 hp at 6000 rpm and 290 ft-lb at 4300 rpm, it could, advised Ford,

1970 Boss 302

1971 Mach I

**1972 Mustang**

"be tuned for more."

Rounding out the Boss 302 formula for motoring fanatics were components that included a 10.4 inch high-capacity clutch, a four-speed gearbox with Hurst shifter, 16:1 steering and Ford's competition handling package of stronger springs, shocks (staggered at the rear) plus front and rear stabilizer bars. A "Daytona" 3.50:1 rear axle was standard but a Traction-Lok differential, with ratios of 3.50, 3.91 and 4.30:1, was optional as was a rear spoiler, backlight louvers, power steering and chrome-plated 15x7 styled steel wheels. Standard on all Boss 302s were seven-inch steel wheels with F60x15 fiberglass-belted tires. Stopping power was provided by 11.3-inch front disc and 10-inch rear drum brakes.

While the Boss 302's existence could be explained by the obvious need to have a Mustang capable of answering the challenge of the Camaro Z/28, its inspiration was the Trans-Am Mustang. The other half of the Boss family, the Boss 429, existed only to allow Ford's crescent V-8 to participate legally in NASCAR competition. Ford described the Boss 429 as "an earth-shaking

**1973 Mustang**

1974 Mustang

1975 Mustang II

1976 Mustang

Following pages, 1977 Cobra II

**1978 Mustang**

combination of big-bore engine and Trans-Am body." Others would call it rare (only 858 were produced in 1969) or expensive (with mandatory options it retailed at $4,798). However, no one ever dared call a Boss 429 dull. As was the Boss 302, the Boss 429 was available only in the Mustang Sportsroof body style, which responded well to the no-nonsense Boss appointments, such as a large hood scoop, front spoiler and seven-inch chrome Magnum 500 wheels.

The first 279 Boss 429 Mustangs had what Ford identified as the S version engine, which was equipped with hydraulic lifters and forged rods. Subsequent models had the T version, which used different rods and pistons and was produced in both hydraulic and solid lifter form. The 429 engine carried four-bolt bearing caps on main bearings numbers one through four, and was fitted with aluminum cylinder heads and intake manifold. Carburetion was by a 735 cfm Holley four-barrel. The only transmission available to handle the Boss 429's obviously understated 375 hp at 5200 rpm and 450 ft-lb of torque at 3400 rpm was a close-ratio four-speed manual linked up to a standard 3.91:1 Traction-Lok differential. An engine oil cooler was standard, as were power brakes (11.3-inch discs up front) and steering, plus a trunk-mounted battery.

The Boss 429 suspension was essentially that of the Cobra Jet with a number of detail changes. Among the most obvious were upper and lower A-arms moved farther outboard, along with even stiffer front springs. Even at its relatively high price (for that day), "Car Life" (July, 1969) concluded that the Boss 429 had "to be the bargain of the year."

The limited availability of the Boss 429 restricted its impact upon the muscle car field, a fate that did not befall the Mach I Mustang. Ford proudly proclaimed the Mach I as a "wild newcomer," and with a standard (and nonfunctional) domed hood spoiler, six-inch styled steel wheels, racing mirrors, pin-type hood latches and high-back bucket seats, it certainly looked the part.

Although the Mach I's base engine was a relatively mild 351 V-8 with a two-barrel carburetor and 9.5:1 compression ratio developing 250 hp at 4600 rpm and 355 ft-lb at 2600 rpm, there were four considerably stronger optional engines. With a four-barrel carburetor and 10.7:1 compression ratio, the 351 Cleveland V-8 pumped out 290 hp at 4800 rpm and 385 ft-lb at 3200 rpm. In its last year as a Mustang engine, the 390 V-8 was the final step prior to reaching the 428 Cobra Jet engine plateau for the Mach I. In the latter form, the Mach I received plaudits from "Car Life" (March, 1969) as the "best Mustang yet and quickest ever." With Cruise-O-Matic, the 428 Mach could cover the quarter-mile in 13.90 seconds—103.32 mph. Mach Is, with the 351 or 390 engine, were equipped with the GT handling package. Those powered by the 428 V-8 received the competition suspension. The same engines offered for the Mach I were also available for Mustangs equipped with the GT Equipment Group, which included styled steel wheels, wide-oval belted whitewalls, simulated hood scoop, NASCAR type hood locks, the special handling package, and body racing stripes. From this dizzy height of power, exciting looks, seemingly endless lists of optional performance features and what we all thought was a never-ending stream of ever-larger V-8 engines, the Mustang maintained a steady course until the early seventies. The

1978 Cobra II

1979 Mustang

Following pages, 1979 Mustang

OFFICIAL PACE CAR
63rd. ANNUAL INDIANAPOLIS 500 MILE RACE MAY 27,1979

MUSTANG
FORD
1979
INDIANAPOLIS MOTOR SPEEDWAY

**1980 Cobra**

Boss 302 was replaced by the Boss 351 in 1971, only to be eliminated, along with all 429 engines, the following year. Representing the sole remaining link with the great Mustang V-s in 1972 was the 351HO, which retained most of the essential performance components of the Boss 351 in conjunction with a 8.8:1 compression ratio. For the Mustang's last year , (1973) prior to downsizing its top engine, the 351 CJ, in spite of a modest 7.9:1 compression ratio, was credited with as much as 264 hp.

The years of the Mustang II (1974-1978) are seen today as a time of transition. The little Mustang was a car fun to drive and in its own way an automobile with more than a few interesting variations, such as the King Cobra and Cobra II. But the year when the Mustang really took that bend in the road leading back to its roots was 1979. The flirtations of the Mustang II with performance were left behind as the Mustang took on a resized and revitalized form. The expensive ($570) TRX suspension option served notice that the new Mustang's image would include a reputation for fine handling, while the 140 hp/302 V-8 and turbocharged 2.3 liter four-cylinder engine suggested that heavy breathing V-8s and perky, European-type engines would be cohabiting back in the old Mustang corral.

Happily this proved to be exactly what Ford had in mind. After a one-year (1982) absence, the 302 V-8 returned in 1981 in HO (High Output) form with 157 hp at 4200 rpm and 247 ft-lb of torque at 2400 rpm. Two years later, in a renaissance of performance that seemed impossible just a few years earlier, the 302 V-8, with a Holley four-barrel and 175 hp, was a key element of the Mustang GT. This horsepower output was matched by the 1984 Mustang SVO. Although its 2.4-liter, sohc four-cylinder engine was in form far removed from the five-liter, 205 hp High Output V-8 of the GT Mustang, the SVO received international recognition as a world class sports car. Meanwhile, the classic performance, so closely linked with the great Mustangs of the sixties, became a hallmark of the Mustang GT.

For 1985, these two exciting engines became even more so. The SVO moved up to a 200 hp rating, while

**1980 Mustang**

**1981 Mustang**

the Mustang GT stepped out with 210 hp at 4600 rpm and 265 ft-lb of torque at 3400 rpm. The result is an automobile capable of seven-second, zero to 60 mph runs.

In the case of the Mustang, the past can be savored without berating the present. Today's Mustang not only bears its name with pride but also gives new meaning to the performance heritage. It's been said before, but let's say it one more time: "The Boss is back"—and we're glad!

**1981 Cobra**

**Following pages, 1982 Mustang**

# This Ford Chases

Over the past eighteen years, Ford Mustang has earned the reputation as one of America's favorite sports cars.

This year, when California's Highway Patrol needed a fleet of 400 high-performance, special pursuit vehicles to help keep their highways safe, 1982 Mustangs got the job.

This pursuit Mustang, powered by a 5.0 liter, high-output engine, accelerates from zero to 50 in 6.3 seconds.

# Porsches For A Living.

Mustang's rack and pinion steering, MacPherson struts, coil springs and anti-sway bar provide the kind of responsive, precise and safe road handling needed in pursuit operations.

In short, Ford Mustang means total driving performance.

There could be a Mustang in your future, too. Even if you don't chase Porsches for a living.

Ford

## There's A Ford In America's Future.

1983 Mustang

1983 Mustang GLX

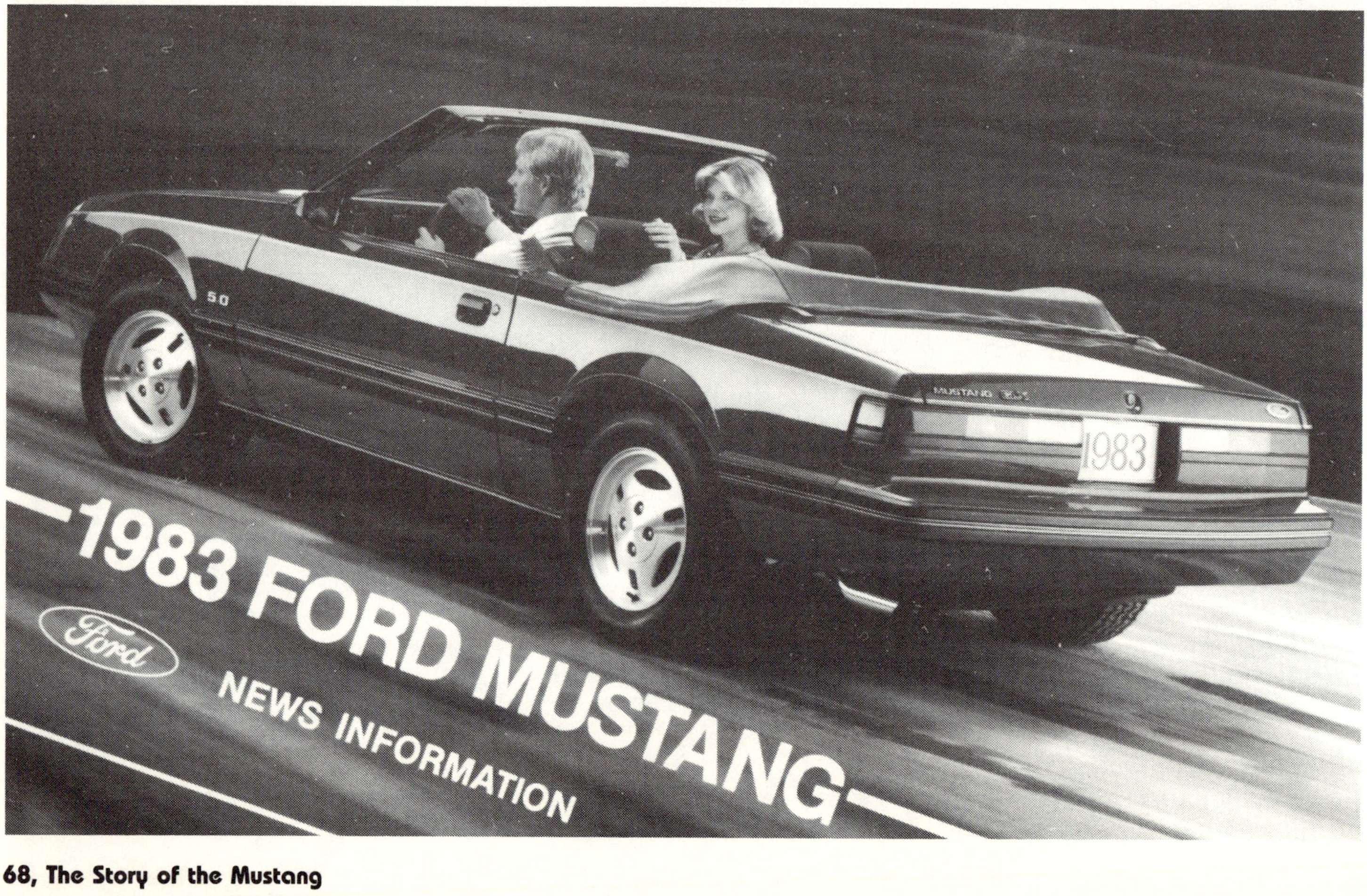

1983 FORD MUSTANG

Ford

NEWS INFORMATION

# A legend turns 20.

Get it together — Buckle up.

# The 20th Anniversary Mustang

Twenty years ago the first Mustang rolled off the assembly line and made automotive history. The fun and excitement of that first year made Mustang a legend.

Now you can capture the spirit of the original in a limited edition Mustang GT. Available in convertible and 3-door models.

**She's quick.**

With a high output 5.0 liter V-8 engine. Five-speed gearbox. And six-way articulated driving seats.

**She's fun.**

Push a button, take a ride with the wind. The convertible has a real glass rear window, room for four and a power top.

**She's rare.**

Only 5,000 Limited Edition Mustangs will be built, so see your dealer soon. And ask about special Anniversary savings on selected Ford cars and trucks.

A sporty car makes it fun. But only Ford makes it Mustang.

The 20th Anniversary Mustang.

**Have you driven a Ford... lately?**

Ford

# Ponycars to GO!
# The Shelby Mustangs.

By Robert C. Ackerson

It was virtually a foregone conclusion that if Carroll Shelby ever got his hands on a Ford Mustang the result would be sensational. After all, what else could be expected from the man who created the Cobra from a dated British two-liter sports car and a sedate Ford V-8 passenger car engine? But it's doubtful that anyone back in the mid-sixties was prepared for a series of automobiles that were more than the Mustang's alter ego. What we got instead were a half-dozen years of pure performance wapped up in packages that were instantly identified at rest and difficult to catch on the run.

The initial GT350 of 1965 used the Ford fastback body with a Wimbledon White finish and Guardsman Blue lower body striping, headlined by GT350 figures. Other attention grabbers included a grille whose only ornamentation was a small Mustang logo, a fiberglass hood with air scoop, plus NASCAR-type pin and dowel hood locks. A base price of $4,547 included an impressive array of performance equipment for what was strictly a two-seater sports car. The GT350 engine was a 289HP V-8 with a 715 cfm Holley four-barrel carburetor, high-rise aluminum manifold, a 10.0:1 compression and welded tube headers. The result was 306 hp at 6000 rpm and 329 lb-ft of torque at 4200 rpm. To handle the vigorous life- style GT350s were expected to have, a 6.5-quart finned and baffled aluminum oil pan was fitted. The only transmission available was a fully-synchronized Borg Warner "Sebring" close-ratio four-speed, with a lightweight all-alloy case. Suspension components included a one-inch diameter front anti-roll bar, rear trailing arms and Koni adjustable shocks

**1966 Shelby G.T.350**

**1968 Shelby G.T.500 KR**

for all four wheels. Other standard features included a "No-Spin" limited slip differential, 15-inch diameter steel wheels (Shelby aluminum wheels were also available for $273.00) carrying 130 mph rated Goodyear "High Performance - Blue Dot" tires and Kelsey Hayes front disc brakes with metallic liners. A special instrument cluster with tachometer and oil pressure gauges in addition to the usual instrumentation was fitted, as was a wood rim racing steering wheel that controlled the 19:1 quick ratio steering.

With a curb weight of approximately 2,800 lbs (distributed in a 53/47 front/rear proportion), the GT350 accelerated from zero to 60 mph in 5.7 seconds, a time which equalled that of the legendary 1957 fuel-injected Corvette. Its ability to accelerate from zero to 100 mph in 14.5 seconds was an achievement that had been expected only of competition sports cars just a few years earlier. Shelby credited the GT350 with a top speed of 133 mph.

Shelby American also offered a "for competition only" GT350 with numerous modifications and racing-oriented features for $5,950.00. A small sampling of its attributes included an engine cooler, electric fuel pump, magnesium 7x15-inch bolt-on wheels, roll bar, plastic rear window and sliding side windows and a "full Shelby American competition prepared and dyno-tuned engine."

Since production of the Shelby Mustangs was always relatively low, numerous changes took place within model year delineations. For example, during the 1968 model run, the GT350's lower A-arm pivot, Koni shocks and override rear traction bars were replaced by standard Mustang pivot positions, American-made heavy-duty shocks and Traction Master bars. Easily distinguishing the 1966 model (except for a few early cars with the 1965 body) were rear quarter panel windows and lower body-mounted air scoops for the rear brakes. A number of new exterior finishes, including Candy Apple Red, Ivy Green and Raven Black, were available. The GT350 engine was unchanged for 1966, but for an additional $670 Shelby would install a Paxton supercharger which, if the normal GT350 was the "fastest production American stock car on the road," qualified it as one of the fastest production stock cars on any country's road.

Although none were supercharged, the 936 cars Shelby-American provided to the Hertz Car Rental Company as the GT350-H models made renting a car an unforgettable experience for many Hertz customers. There were subtle differences between the GT350 and the H version, but none of them diluted the GT350's pure performance theme. Initially, the Hertz cars were set apart by their jet black body and twin gold rally stripes running from the grille to the rear bumper. As the production run continued, the GT350-H was offered in the same colors as the GT350.

The introduction of a restyled Mustang for 1967 obviously was a tough act for Ford, since it didn't want to lose the Mustang's essence for the mere sake of change. But for Carroll Shelby, a new Mustang was no source of worry; it was just another opportunity to create more great automobiles! Moreover, Ford was sizing up the Mustang to compete in the supercar class and the result was a running mate to the GT350 known as the GT500. Except for interior and exterior identification, these two cars were identical in appearance. Shelby used a simple grille opening with inboard-mounted dual 7 inch running lights, a fiberglass front hood and nose section and, as expected, plenty of body striping.

Modifications to the stock Mustang suspension included stiffer springs, Gabriel tubular shocks and a larger 0.94-inch front stabilizer bar. Goodyear Speedway, E70-15 blackwall tires with a 140 mph rating were standard. The GT350 engine, still available with the Paxton supercharged option was, except for its stock Mustang cast-iron exhaust manifolds, unchanged from previous years. The GT500 engine was Ford's 428 cid V-8 with hydraulic lifters, dual-point distributor, twin Holley, 600 cfm, four-barrel carburetors on an aluminum high-rise manifold and a 10.5:1 compression ratio. Its power ratings were 355 hp at 5400 rpm and 420 lb-ft at 3200 rpm. A very few GT500s were also constructed with specially built 427 cid V-8 engines.

The purpose for which the GT350 and GT500 were intended was simple. "They are," said Shelby-

## THE DIFFERENCE BETWEEN THE SHELBY G.T. 350 AND THE MUSTAN

**1** The cast aluminum high-rise manifold increases the engine's ability to breathe Holley low-restriction four-barrel carburetor with center pivot floats which prevent aluminum Cobra rocker covers have excellent sound deadening qualities. **3** The surge during hard cornering, acceleration or braking. **4** The Borg Warner special ability of the engine is improved further by the use of hand-made steel tube exhaust wheel upper control arms are moved down one inch improving cornering power cornering ability. **8** Monte Carlo reinforcing bar plus extra heavy reinforcing yoke reaction arms are added to take the burden of acceleration and braking forces and Hayes disc brakes are added with ventilated discs and special full competition is practically fade-free. Special wheels are mounted with 130 mph-rated Goodyear **12** Overall steering ratio is reduced from 21:1 to 19:1. **13** Competition-type locking

**OPTIONS:** Shelby aluminum wheels; "No-spin" limited slip differential; Compet

**...plenty!**

at high speeds and extends its useful power range. Matched to the manifold is a
flooding or fuel starvation under the most severe driving conditions. **2** Custom
Cobra cast and finned oil pan increases oil capacity, aids cooling and prevents oil
Sebring close ratio four speed transmission is fully synchronized. **5** The breathing
headers and low restriction, straight-through mufflers. **6** Inner pivots of the front
and bite. **7** Full one inch diameter anti-roll bar further increases roll stiffness and
add body stability and strength under severe driving conditions. **9** A pair of torque
allow the springs to handle the weight of the car effectively. **10** At the front, Kelsey
pads. At the rear, the G.T. 350 has 10" drums with metallic linings. This combination
low profile high performance tires. **11** Heavy duty shock absorbers are adjustable.
studs and safety pins eliminate danger of the hood ever flying open at high speeds.

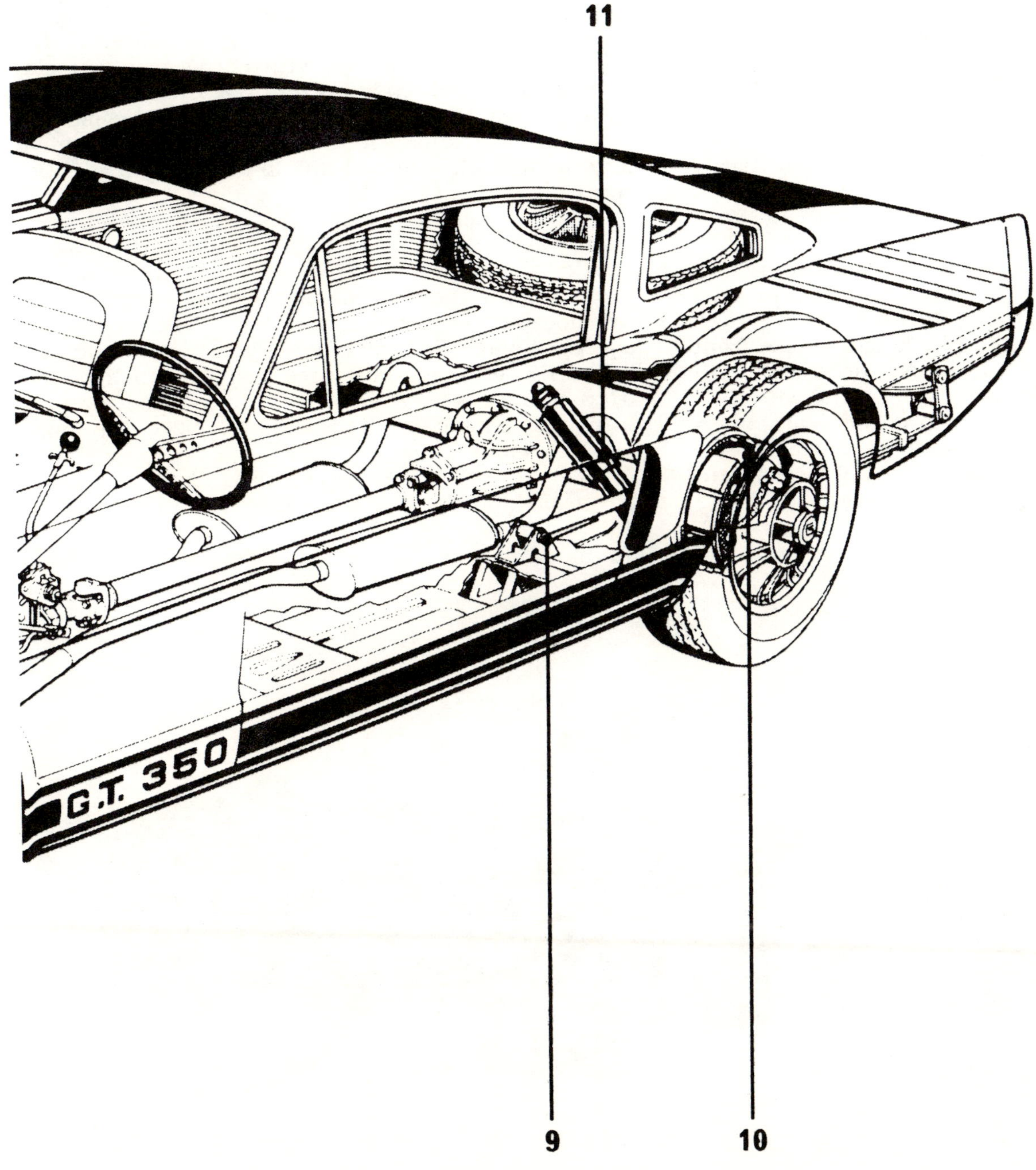


:ition striping; Automatic transmission; Folding rear seat.

American, "true GT (gran turismo) cars, capable of transporting four people, or two people and a large quantity of luggage, long distances at high average speeds." Obviously there was an informed, intelligent and enthusiastic group of Americans who were looking for exactly this type of automobile, since 1,175 GT350s and 2,050 GT500s were produced during 1967.

In 1968, Shelby adopted the Cobra name for his gran touring cars, identifying them as the Shelby Cobra GT350 and the Shelby Cobra GT500. Changes for 1968 were far more substantial than just a couple of name changes, however. For the first time a convertible, complete with a roll bar, was offered as an alternative to the fastback body style. The 271 hp-289 cid V-8 was no longer offered by Ford and, in its place, the GT350 was powered by a 302 cid V-8 with hydraulic lifters, a 600 cfm Holley four-barrel carburetor and an aluminum intake manifold. Peak horsepower was 250 at 4800 rpm. Maximum torque was 310 lb-ft at 2800 rpm. This engine could also be equipped with the Paxton supercharger. The GT500 base engine was Ford's 428 cid V-8 equipped with cylinder heads that had originated with the 427 cid V-8 used by Ford in NASCAR competition. With a 715 cfm Holley four-barrel carburetor, its peak horsepower was 360. Available, but rarely seen, was the 427 cid Ford V-8 with 400 hp at 5600 rpm and 460 lb-ft of torque at 3200.

Regardless of their engines, the Shelby Cobra GTs were exciting to look at. At the rear were sequential taillights borrowed from the 1965 Thunderbird, as well as a rear spoiler carrying Shelby lettering. The front end appearance was dominated by a hood with twin scoops, plus a low and wide grille opening with dual rectangular Lucas lights. As in previous years, fiberglass was used for the hood and front grille panels.

When Ford introduced the 428 cid Cobra Jet late in the 1968 model year, Shelby quite logically used it for a new model, the GT500-KR, which superseded the GT500. In Cobra Jet form, the 428 engine used the cylinder heads and manifolds from the 427 cid NASCAR engine, a 735 cfm Holley four-barrel carburetor and was credited with a 10.6:1 compression ratio. However, its horsepower rating was conservative, 335 at 5200 rpm. Peak torque was 440 lb-ft at 3400 rpm.

The final two years of Shelby GT production were spectacular. All-new Mustang styling enabled Shelby to revamp his cars with new fiberglass body panels, such as a triple-scoop hood. A full-width front grille encompassed the twin headlights and inboard-mounted rectangular running lights. The rear deck carried a prominent spoiler which, along with rectangular taillights, exhaust exits and Shelby lettering, gave the Shelby GTs instant identification. The only engine available for the GT500 was the 335 hp 428 Cobra Jet. The base engine for the GT350 was a very mild 302 V-8 with 220 hp at 4600 rpm and 300 lb-ft at 2600 rpm. However, the GT350 was also available with Ford's new 351 cid Cleveland V-8 which, like the 428 Cobra Jet, was equipped with Ram Air induction. Its 10.7:1 compression ratio and Autolite four-barrel carburetor provided 290 hp at 4800 rpm and 385 lb-ft of torque at 3400 rpm.

Both models had the Mustang heavy-duty suspension system with large 1.37-inch Ford Adjust-O-Matic shocks. Those on the GT500 were mounted on opposite sides of the rear axle, while those on the GT350 were located in conventional fashion. Both types were equipped with 15x7 inch mag-type wheels, Goodyear belted E70x15 wide oval tires and 11.3 inch power front disc brakes. A close-ratio four-speed manual transmission was standard for the GT500 and optional for the GT350.

The final 1970 versions of the GT350 and GT500 physically differed from their 1969 counterparts only

**1966 Shelby G.T.350 H**

**1967 Shelby G.T.350**

by virtue of their black hood stripes and black plastic front spoilers. However, the standard engine for the GT350 was the Ram Air 351 cid V-8.

The Shelby GTs were always uncommon cars in an automotive age that by any measure was exceptional. Created by a man whose business acumen was tempered by an awareness of what high performance was all about, they left the scene at the peak of their proficiency as grand touring automobiles. As such, their impact upon automotive history was far greater than their low production totals would suggest. They made their mark, not by setting sales records, but by setting new standards of performance excellence for the American automobile.

# SHELBY G.T. 350 / G.T. 500 POWERED BY FORD

## GENERAL SPECIFICATIONS:
## GT 350 and GT 500

Wheelbase ............................108.0"
Tread ....................Front, 58.0"; Rear, 58.0"
Length ..............................186.6"
Width ...............................70.9"
Height ..............................51.6"
Curb weight ....GT 350, 2723 lbs.; GT 500, 3286 lbs.
Distribution, front/rear:
GT 500: 56.4% F, 43.6% R
GT 350: 53.0% F, 47.0% R
Body type ......................2-door fastback

**CONSTRUCTION:** Platform type unitized construction with reinforced floor side members and export front end reinforcement.

**STYLING:** Front; 3.0" extended reinforced fiberglas nose, custom grille with 30% more frontal cooling area. Quad headlights, highbeams inset in grille. Custom fiberglas hood with sculptured airscoop. LeMans locking pins. Sides; functional brake airscoops set in rear quarter sculpturing, LeMans air extractors in rear quarters of roof. Rear; sculptured air spoiler across rear deck, full-width taillights. Side striping with model designation above rocker panels.

**SUSPENSION:** Front; independent, with coil springs and ball joints, Shelby-modified for flatter cornering. .94" diameter front stabilizer bar. Rear; 4-leaf springs with special rebound dampers to control rear spring windup.

**SPRING RATES:**
500: 360 lbs./in. front, 135 lbs./in. rear
350: 320 lbs./in. front, 135 lbs./in. rear

**SHOCK ABSORBERS:** Tubular, heavy-duty adjustable, factory preset for most driving conditions.

**TRANSMISSION:** Fully synchronized four-speed manual (31 spline for 500, 28 spline for 350) standard.

**Ratios:** First — 2.32:1, Second — 1.69:1, Third — 1.29:1, Top — 1.00:1, Reverse — 2.32:1

**Heavy-duty Cruise-O-Matic transmission optional.** Shift handle lockout prevents skipping or missed shifts when hand-selecting gears.

**Ratios:** First — 2.46:1, Second — 1.46:1, Top — 1.00:1, Reverse — 2.20:1

**FINAL DRIVE:** Heavy-duty rear axle with straddle-mounted deep offset drive pinion. Standard ratios:

**500** — Manual transmission 3.50:1
Automatic transmission 3.25:1

**350** — Manual transmission 3.89:1
Automatic transmission 3.50:1

**STEERING:** Recirculating ball and nut, linkage-type power assist provides crisp 16-to-1 overall steering ratio, 37.16 foot turning diameter.

**WHEELS, TIRES:** Shelby 15" steel wheel with 6.5" rim width. "Speedway 350" low profile 4-ply nylon E70-15 tires designed especially for Shelby GT cars.

**BRAKES:** Front; disc, 11.3", with high speed linings. Rear; 10" x 2.5" cast iron drum, self adjusting. 191.0 sq. in. effective lining area. Independent service brake operating rear drum brakes.

**INTERIOR APPOINTMENTS:** Deluxe interior with front bucket seats, sculptured folding rear seat* providing carpeted luggage deck. Full instrumentation including 8000 rpm tachometer, 140 mph speedometer, ammeter, oil pressure, water temperature, fuel, Integral roll bar* (meets competition requirements). Inertia reel front shoulder harnesses*, seat belts front and rear, padded dashboard and sun visors.

These specifications and options were in effect at the time of printing. In the interest of constant product improvement, Shelby American, Inc. reserves the right to add, alter or delete equipment or options, or to change specifications at any time without notice and without incurring obligation.

*Optional at extra cost

# GT 350/GT 500-KR

## GENERAL SPECIFICATIONS

**DIMENSIONS**

**Body types:** 2-door fastback and convertible. Full unitized construction.
**Wheelbase:** 108.0"
**Tread:** Front, 58.1"; Rear 58.1"
**Length:** 186.81"
**Width:** 70.9"
**Height:** Fastback, 51.8"
**††Curb weight:**
350 (302 engine, autom. transm.); fastback 3146 lbs.
500-KR (428 engine, autom. transm.); fastback, 3460 lbs.
**††Weight distribution:** 350: 53% F, 47% R.
**(Fastback)** 500-KR: 56.4% F, 43.6% R.
††Estimated design weights

**SUSPENSION**

**Front:** Independent with coil springs and ball joints. Spring rates; 320 lbs./in. (350), 360 lbs./in. (500-KR). Front stabilizer bar, .94" diameter. Extra capacity telescopic double acting tubular adjustomatic shock absorbers.
**Rear:** 4-leaf semi-elliptic springs with extra capacity telescopic double acting tubular adjustomatic shock absorbers.
**Rate:** 135 lbs./in. (350 and 500-KR).
**Steering:** Recirculating ball and nut with hydraulic power assist. Steering ratio 16:1; 37.16' turning circle.

**BRAKES, WHEELS, TIRES**

**Brakes:** Front, floating caliper power assisted ventilated 11.3" discs with high performance pads; rear drums 10" x 1.75" size with high performance linings. Dual master cylinder with low pressure warning light. Effective lining area: 180.0 sq. in.

**Wheels:** 15" safety type steel wheel, 6" rim width with diecast cover standard.

**Tires:** All new 15" Goodyear E70 polyglass wide path tires are designed for this car, 130 mph test standard.

**TRANSMISSIONS, FINAL DRIVE**

**Transmission:** Fully synchronized four-speed manual standard.
Ratios: First—2.32:1
Second—1.69:1
Third—1.29:1
Top—1.00:1
Reverse—2.32:1
Heavy-duty close-coupled automatic transmission optional. Shift handle detent minimizes skipping or missed shifts when hand-selecting gears.
Ratios: First—2.46:1
Second—1.46:1
Top—1.00:1
Reverse—2.20:1

**Final Drive:** Heavy-duty rear axle with straddle-mounted large diameter ring gear and deep offset drive pinion. Torque-sensitive locking rear† standard on GT 500-KR.
Standard ratios:
500-KR—Manual transmission 3.50:1
Automatic transmission 3.50:1
Options: 3.00:1, 4.11:1, 4.25:1, 4.56:1*
350—Manual transmission 3.89:1
Automatic transmission 3.50:1
Options: 4.11:1, 4.56:1*

**SAFETY FEATURES**

Padded instrument panel, steering wheel center, sun visors. Impact-absorbing collapsible steering column. Seat back retaining latches, padded front seat backs, safety door and regulator handles. Seat belts front and rear. Advanced design front seat shoulder harnesses with improved inertia reels (dual style in fastback, diagonal style in convertible). Padded high-strength steel 1½" diameter integral overhead safety bar. Sequential turn signals, front safety marker lights, rear quarter marker reflectors.

**STYLING APPOINTMENTS**

**Exterior:** Precision moulded custom fiberglass hood and front assembly incorporates dual air intake scoops, functional louvered extractors. Custom self retained push-and-turn hood locks. Separately circuited rectangular fog lights mounted in grille opening. Rolled section lightweight moldings on grille. Le Mans type air extractors on rear quarters of roof (fastback only). Brake air scoops set in lower rear quarters. Precision moulded custom fiberglass trunk deck lid with integral air spoiler. New KR identification in GT stripe on lower rocker panels.

**Interior:** Deluxe all-vinyl interior with bucket seats, full loop pile carpeting, matching custom styled console with padded arm-rest glove box, walnut-grained appliques on instrument panel and door panels. Real wood shift knobs. Full instrumentation; 8000 rpm tachometer, 140 mph speedometer, oil pressure, ammeter, water temperature, fuel gauge, electric clock. Folding rear seat* (fastback only). Tie-down loops for skis or surfboard on safety bar (convertible only).

These specifications were in effect at the time of printing. In the interest of constant product improvement, Shelby Automotive, Inc. reserves the right to add, alter or delete equipment or options, or to change specifications at any time without notice and without incurring obligation.

*Extra-cost option †Except with air-conditioning

**THESE FEATURES GIVE THE SHELBY COBRA GT ITS UNIQUE CHARACTER**

Many of these features give the Cobra GT its exciting look—but the subtle engineering that you do not see is what you appreciate the more you drive this great car. (1) Performance is exciting with either of these two GT models. GT 350, 250 hp 302 cu. in. V-8; GT 500-KR, 335 hp 428 cu. in. all new Cobra Jet V-8. Each engine features (2) high velocity, high volume Cobra intake manifold, (3) advanced design 4-barrel carburetion, (4) dual exhausts, (5) low restriction custom paper-element diecast aluminum air cleaner. (Ram air package standard on GT 500-KR). Every engine looks the part, too, with (6) die cast aluminum Cobra rocker cover, chromed filler cap, dipstick. Handling response is immediate under all conditions, thanks to (7) high-rate front coil spring, (8) high capacity heavy-duty adjustomatic shock absorbers front and rear, (9) .94" diameter front stabilizer bar, (10) crisp 16.0:1 steering ratio with power assist, (11) heavy duty four-leaf rear springs with (12) anti-windup dampers for sure acceleration, (13) heavy-duty rear axle. Tires and brakes match the GT's performance. (14) Power-assisted floating caliper front disc and (15) heavy duty rear drum brakes work with (16) Goodyear E70 polyglass tires and (17) 6" rim width 15" safety wheels for utmost safety. Other safety items include (18) inertia-reel shoulder harnesses and seat belts for front-seat passengers (seat belts in rear), (19) integral overhead safety bar in all models, (20) safety-sequence wide tail lights, (21) front marker lights and (22) rear quarter reflectors, (23) rectangular fog lights and (24) dual master brake cylinder with proportioning valve and low-pressure warning light, (25) collapsible steering column, safety padded steering wheel, (26) full unitized chassis and body.

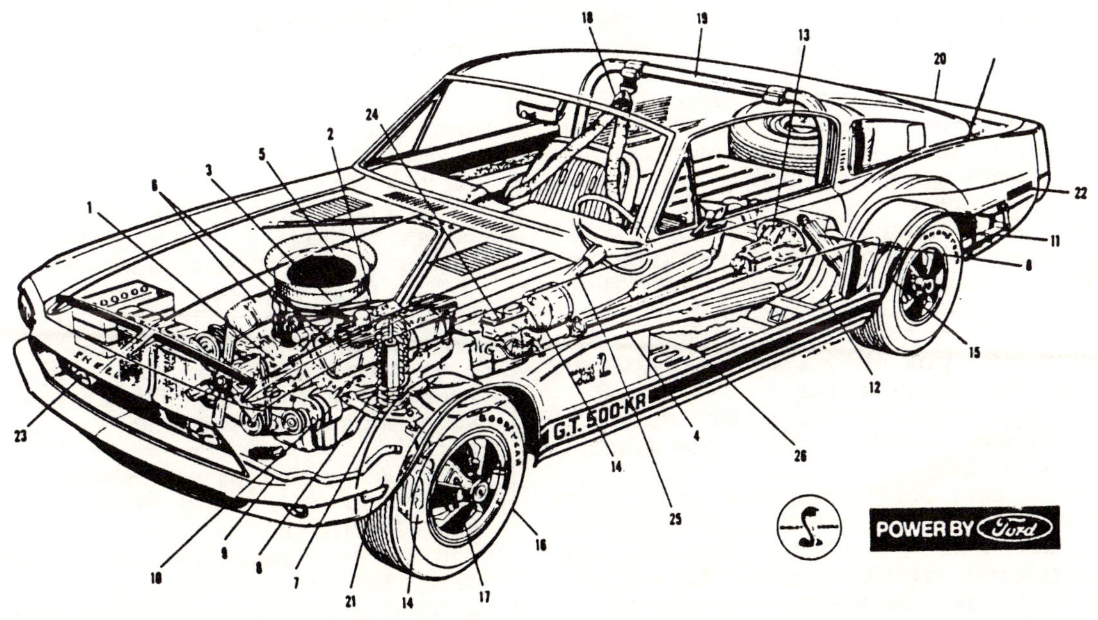

# On the Circuit: 1984 Racing Review.

## 1983

## JANUARY

At the start of the new year, Ford Motorsport wasted no time in announcing an ambitious racing program for 1983.

The emphasis was on private teams competing independently, making the Ford Motorsport program different from any before it.

The only direct corporate involvement by Ford would come in the Camel GT series with Mustang Turbos and, later in the year, the new Mustang GTPs, driven by Bobby Rahal, Geoff Brabham, Tim CoConis and Klaus Ludwig.

On the NASCAR circuit, Ford Thunderbirds would be driven by Dale Earnhardt (built by Bud Moore), Buddy Baker (Wood Brothers), Bill Elliott (Melling Racing) and Dick Brooks (Junie Donlavey.)

In the SCCA Trans-Am series, it was Tom Gloy and Lyn St. James in a pair of Lane Sports Mercury Capris and Vern Smith in another Capri.

Another entry in the IMSA Camel GT series would be Bruce Jenner and John Bauer in a Brooks Racing GTO-class Mustang.

In drag racing, Bob Glidden and Rickie Smith started off with new Pro Stock Thunderbirds while Roy Hill was in a Mercury Capri. In Funny Cars, it was Raymond Beadle in his Blue Max Ford EXP and Kenny Bernstein in his Budweiser King Mercury LN7.

## FEBRUARY

The NASCAR Ford Thunderbirds burst on the scene in February in one of the most thrilling Daytona 500s ever.

Four of the five Thunderbirds in the race had a turn at leading the 500, and they were up front for a total of 58 laps.

Buddy Baker pulled into the lead with 12 laps to go and ended up finishing third, while Bill Elliott sneaked in for second place and Dick Brooks finished fifth.

The fourth member of the T-bird contingent, Dale Earnhardt, led the prized seventh lap of the 500 to collect the $7,011 bonus from 7-Eleven.

Drag racing's Rickie Smith wasn't so lucky in February. His Pro Stock Thunderbird was stolen from his hotel after he had won the first round of eliminations at the NHRA Winternationals. The rig was recovered but all that was left was the car and its two spare engines. All the special tools and parts were gone.

The Winternationals went better for Bob Glidden, and he posted a record qualifying time in his Pro Stock Thunderbird.

In Miami, a rainstorm soaked the Miami Grand Prix and dampened the Ford Mustang Turbo team's chance for a victory in the IMSA Camel GT event.

## MARCH

The Formula 1 season got underway in March, and the Ford-Cosworth engine proved it was still very much alive and well.

It was, in fact, a huge factor in the Brazilian Grand Prix.

Keke Rosberg put his Williams-Ford on the pole, and three of the top six finishers in the race were powered by Ford. Niki Lauda finished third in a McLaren, Jacques Lafitte was fourth in a Williams and Marc Surer came in sixth in an Arrows.

Rosberg would have made it four out of six for Ford but his second-place finish was disqualified for an illegal push-start.

Ford-powered cars kept rolling, and after the second race of the season, eight of the 11 cars scoring championship points were powered by the Ford-Cosworth DFVs.

John Watson and Niki Lauda finished 1-2 in a pair of McLaren Fords at the Grand Prix of Long Beach. Lafitte, Surer and Johnny Cecotto went 4-5-6.

Also in March, Bill Elliott moved to the top of the NASCAR points list, but he was frustrated with another second-place finish.

The Melling Ford Thunderbird driver came within .78 seconds of gaining his first NASCAR win when he finished half a car length behind Richard Petty at the rain-delayed Carolina 500.

## APRIL

Tom Gloy looked into his crystal ball in April and predicted his Lane Sports Mercury Capri would finish at the top of the Trans-Am standings.

And while he finished 26th in the first race of the season at Moroso Motorsport Park, he remained optimistic largely due to the pole position he earned in qualifying and the ease with which he led the early laps before a tire blew.

After the first two Trans-Am races of '83, Gloy had set two qualifying records and was runner-up at Summit Point. His teammate, Lyn St. James, finished eighth. In the opener at Moroso she staged a strong comeback to finish 18th.

In off-road racing, Josele Garza picked up a win in the first of Mickey Thompson's four-event Gran Prix series. Garza drove a Ford Ranger to victory in the Grand National Pickup class at the Los Angeles race.

Bruce Jenner and John Bauer were impressive in their first two races in the Brooks Racing Ford Mustang, but new-car demons made it frustrating at times.

Jenner and Bauer finished eighth in their debut at the 6-hour Los Angeles Times Grand Prix. In the next race at Laguna Seca Raceway, Bauer was closing in on the lead early in the race when the Mustang was knocked off the course.

In spite of the disappointments, the Mustang showed tremendous potential in its first two outings. In an unofficial practice at Riverside, Bauer lapped the 3.3-mile road course within a hair of the existing Camel GTO qualifying record.

## MAY

The Ford Mustang Turbos provided a performance worthy of an encore at the Monterey Camel GT race on May 1. But instead it marked a spectacular end to a 15-race career.

Bobby Rahal made a daring move at the start of the race, darting past pole-winner Al Holbert. And after Rahal was forced to take a penalty stop, he charged back through the traffic, catching up to teammate Geoff Brabham.

From there the two drivers drive nose-to-tail, putting on a dramatic display of driving until Brabham's car lost a differential oil seal and dropped out with 10 laps to go.

Rahal ended up finishing third as the experimental Mustang Turbos were retired.

At the end of May, the Ford Thunderbird NASCAR team picked up nearly every prize at the World 600 in Charlotte, N.C.

Buddy Baker, Bill Elliott and Dale Earnhardt captured the top three qualifying spots and were separated by just 0.117 mph.

The Bud Moore crew for Earnhardt won the Ingersoll-Rand Proto Tool pit crew competition, just edging Baker's Wood Brothers crew for the award.

Elliott captured the Curtis Turner Memorial Award for the most outstanding performance by a driver other than the winner.

The only thing eluding the Thunderbirds was a first-place finish in the 600.

Earnhardt finished the race fifth while Baker was seventh and Elliott came in 16th.

## JUNE

Ford's new IMSA Mustang GTP grabbed all the attention at Ford Motor Company's second annual Detroit Grand Prix Reception, June 2.

The concept of a front-engined, ground effects race car caught more than a few people by surprise. And many were intrigued by the GTP's carbon fiber chassis and the fact that it was designed and constructed by Ford Aerospace & Communications Corporation (FACC).

In the same week, Ford-Cosworth-powered cars swept the Detroit Grand Prix. Michele Alboreto in a Tyrrell-Ford, Keke Rosberg in a Williams-Ford and John Watson in a McLaren-Ford went 1-2-3.

Also in Ford-powered cars, Jacques Laffite finished fifth and Nigel Mansell was sixth.

Fords were also tearing up the racing world in Columbus, Ohio, in June.

Raymond Beadle and Bob Glidden captured top honors at the NHRA Springnationals, Beadle in his Schlitz Blue Max Ford EXP Funny Car and Glidden in his Pro Stock Ford Thunderbird.

The victories marked an end of personal slumps for both racers.

## JULY

July belonged to Ford Thunderbirds in NASCAR Grand National racing as Dale Earnhardt captured two victories and Buddy Baker earned one.

Baker took the first win of the month when he coasted to the finish line at Daytona in the July 4 Firecracker 400 on an empty gas tank.

It was Baker's first trip to the winner's circle in 1983 after several near misses.

Earnhardt's victories came at the Busch 420 in Nashville, Tenn., and the Talladega 500 at Talladega, Ala.

At Talladega, Ford Thunderbirds were running 1-2-3 at the halfway point of the race. But in the end it came down to just Earnhardt, and he won a thrilling last-lap duel with Darrell Waltrip.

Dick Brooks ended up seventh while Bill Elliott finished eighth.

Another Ford Thunderbird rolled to victory in July, but this time it was Bob Glidden's Pro Stock car. Glidden broke the meet's elapsed time and speed records on the way to victory at the NHRA Mile-High Nationals in Denver, Colo.

The victory was Glidden's 37th National championship.

# AUGUST

Ford's new IMSA Mustang GTP cars made headlines in a big way in August. In their debut at Road America, Aug. 21, one car won and the other came third in the IMSA Camel GT 500-miler.

It was, in a very real sense, the beginning of a new era in the long history of Ford Motor Company's involvement in motor racing.

Tim CoConis and Klaus Ludwig brought their Ford Mustang GTP to victory more than two laps ahead of the second-place finisher, and Bobby Rahal and Geoff Brabham iced the victory cake with a third place in a second Mustang GTP.

For Michael Kranefuss, director of Ford Special Vehicle Operations (SVO), and Bob Riley, SVO designer, the victory proved their theory that a well-engineered, front-engined race car with a small (1.7 liter) turbocharged motor could outrun foreign prototypes with bigger V8s and six-cylinder motors.

It also proved that Ford's much-heralded return to racing was bearing fruit on the international racing scene.

Also in August, Kranefuss was given the added responsibility of coordinating Ford's worldwide motorsport and related activities.

# SEPTEMBER

September opened with a bang for drag racers Kenny Bernstein and Bob Glidden.

Both captured titles at the prestigious U.S. Nationals at Indianapolis over Labor Day weekend. And Bernstein walked off with the biggest paycheck in drag racing history with prize-earnings totaling $80,000.

Glidden drove his Ford Thunderbird to victory in Pro Stock and the win gave him his third straight NHRA National win. He remained in third place on the NHRA points list.

The Mustang GTP's were back on the scene in September, and while they continued to show championship potential, this outing wasn't as satisfying as their Aug. 21 debut.

Geoff Brabham took the lead briefly in one of the GTPs, but both cars dropped out of the Camel GT 500 at Pocono International Raceway.

One car ran out of luck when a stone punched through the protective radiator screen and chewed up the car's turbocharger. The other car went out with a broken valve train.

The IHRA season wrapped up in September with Rickie Smith finishing second in Pro Stock and Raymond Beadle second in Pro Funny Car.

# OCTOBER

The motor racing year began winding down in October, and Tom Gloy found himself in a very familiar place. The Mercury Capri driver placed third in the last Trans-Am race of the season — the Caesars Palace Grand Prix, Oct. 8. And he also finished third in the final Trans-Am standings.

His third in the season finale marked his seventh third-place finish in 12 events this year.

But Gloy said he accomplished a lot of good things in 1983, despite not winning a race.

"Just in the last month we made gains in our engine-development program that were very significant and proved to be important here," he said after the Caesars Palace race.

Gloy's teammate, Lyn St. James, finished 11th in the race and 10th in the final Trans-Am standings.

Vern Smith, in the third Capri, finished 14th on the final list.

Bill Elliott continued to make a run at his first NASCAR victory, but the best he could manage in October was a fourth at the Holly Farms 400. Dale Earnhardt posted a runner-up finish at that race.

The NHRA season wrapped up in October with Bob Glidden finishing third in the final Pro Stock standings, Rickie Smith in seventh and Roy Hill in ninth.

In Funny Car, Kenny Bernstein finished third, Tom Anderson fifth, and Raymond Beadle eighth.

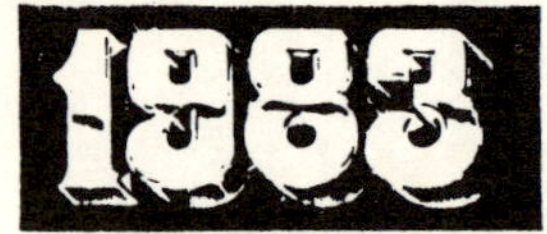

## NOVEMBER

At last, Bill Elliott broke the jinx and captured his first NASCAR victory. The popular Melling Ford Thunderbird driver had recorded eight second-place finishes in his career.

Elliott won the Winston Western 500 on Nov. 20, just days after the Adolph Coors Company announced its new three-year contract with Melling Racing and the Elliott family.

The victory at the Western 500 made Elliott the 12th different Winston Cup winner of the year.

Earlier in the month, Manny Esquerra completed off-road's "triple crown" by winning the rugged Baja 1000. The Ford Ranger driver had won the Mint 400 and Frontier 500 earlier in the season.

Esquerra finished nearly five hours ahead of his nearest competitor in the two-day, 815-mile race.

In November, Zakspeed USA — one of the world's leading auto racing teams and engine developers — opened for business in the United States.

Zakspeed USA officially established headquarters Nov. 14 in the Detroit suburb of Livonia.

Most of Zakspeed USA's plans are tied to the Ford Motorsport program. In 1984, it will continue to prepare and develop two prototype Mustang GTPs for the IMSA Camel GT series.

## DECEMBER

The announcement of a major sponsorship by Southland Corporation's 7-Eleven and Chief Auto Parts stores of a number of Ford teams highlights the month of December.

The sponsor package provides Southland with a presence in almost every form of auto racing, from IMSA and Indy to off-road and amateur Sports Car Club of America events.

It also brings two of America's most promising young racers into the Ford family, Kyle Petty and Billy Meyer, both of whom raced under the 7-Eleven, Chief Auto Parts banners in 1983.

Petty will race a 7-Eleven Ford Thunderbird in the NASCAR Grand National series, while Meyer will drag race a Ford Mustang Funny Car in 1984.

The sponsorship package also encompasses a number of established Ford teams and drivers, including backing of a Mustang GTP for Bobby Rahal and Geoff Brabham, and Mercury Capri for Tom Gloy in Trans-Am racing, both wearing 7-Eleven colors.

Chief Auto Parts is sponsoring a brace of off-road

Rangers which will be driven by Manny Esquerra and Josele Garza, plus Bob Glidden in his drag racing Pro Stock Thunderbird.

Also included is sponsorship of a number of RS-class Ford Escorts and Mercury Lynxes in IMSA racing and an amateur series for SCCA Formula Ford.

# in '84

## JANUARY

Ford Motorsport called 1984 the year to plunge forward, full speed ahead, and that's exactly what it did.

In January, Ford Motorsport announced an expanded program that included associations with racers all the way from the NASCAR circuit to Saturday night short-track racing and everything in between.

Part of that program involved new products for use at all levels of competition.

Michael Kranefuss, director of Ford's Special Vehicle Operations (SVO) said SVO's goal was to make performance equipment "available to everybody who wants to race Fords, be it amateur racing or, or eventually, Formula 1 again."

In another show of commitment toward all levels of racing, Ford announced it would sponsor, with 7-Eleven, the SCCA National Formula Ford series which includes some 1,250 drivers in 71 events.

In professional racing, Ford welcomed several new drivers into the fold, including Kyle Petty and Ricky Rudd on the NASCAR circuit and Billy Meyer in NHRA and IHRA Funny Car competition.

In IMSA Camel GT racing, plans were to run one Ford Mustang GTP for the full schedule and another for six of the 17 races.

There was also the announcement that the Ford Motor Company and Cosworth engineering, already partners for 25 successful years, would combine forces to develop and produce a year 2000 Grand Prix Formula 1 racing engine which is scheduled to make its debut in 1986.

## FEBRUARY

Manny Esquerra made sure Ford's racing season got off to a great start in 1984 with a pair of wins in February.

Esquerra drove his Chief Auto Parts-sponsored Ford Ranger to a season-opening Class 7 win in the SCORE Parker 400, Feb. 4.

It was Esquerra's seventh victory in the last nine Parker 400s, and came in front of many of his family and friends. His home is only 12 miles from the finish line in Parker, Ariz.

Willie Valdez, in a Ford Ranger, won the Class 7s race for stock mini pickups while Dave Shoppe's Class 8 win in his Ford F150 made it a clean sweep for Ford drivers in Parker.

Esquerra ended the month with another Class 7 win, this time at the High Desert Laughlin Desert Challenge in Laughlin, Nev. on Feb. 25.

On the NASCAR circuit, things started out slow, but improved very quickly.

Bill Elliott, who won the last race of 1983, placed fifth in the Daytona 500 on Feb. 19, but his was the highest finish of any Ford driver.

One week later, however, things changed for the better when a battered Ricky Rudd fought his way to a win in the Feb. 26 Miller High Life 400 in Richmond, Va.

The win was even more remarkable considering Rudd was still feeling the effects of a spectacular crash two weeks earlier in the Busch Clash at Daytona.

Rudd collected $31,775 for the win while Elliott, with a fourth-place finish, became 1984's first new member of NASCAR's millionaires club.

Ford also took an early lead in the manufacturer's championship of the Champion Spark Plug Challenge RS series when Craig Ross and Jon Beekhuis drove the 7-Eleven-sponsored Ford Escort to a victory in the front-wheel drive class in the car's debut race at Daytona on Feb. 4.

## MARCH

Kenny Bernstein made sure March would be a month to remember when broke the 260-mph barrier and shattered the world Funny Car top speed record at the NHRA Gatornationals at Gainsville (Fla.) Raceway on March 18.

In his Budweiser King Ford Tempo, Bernstein blasted his way to a 260.11 mph clocking in the finals to beat John Collins.

Bernstein credited his crew chief, Dale Armstrong, and his team's wind-tunnel testing for reaching the 260 mark.

"I think this is just the tip of the iceberg," he said. "I don't think there is a limit."

In off-road racing, Willie Valdez continued his successful start with a Class 7s victory at the SCORE San Felipe 250 in Baja, Cal. on March 25.

The win was Valdez's fourth in six starts on the young season.

Dave Shoppe scored his first victory of the season with his Ford F150 on March 18 in a High Desert Racing Association event at Firebird Lake, Ariz.

At Rockingham, N.C. on March 4, Chameleon Sun Glasses Ford Thunderbird driver Dick Brooks joined Bill Elliott in the NASCAR millionaires club. Brooks led the race for 169 laps before being involved in a collision that sent him into a wall and damaged his steering.

## APRIL

Taking a cue from Kenny Bernstein, Billy Meyer took his Chief Auto Parts-sponsored Ford Mustang in for wind-tunnel testing that paid off in instant results.

Meyer roared to the NHRA Southern Nationals Funny Car championship, ironically topping Bernstein in an all-Ford final on April 15 in Commerce, Ga.

Meyer, who had been in the wind tunnel on the previous Tuesday, scorched the track with a 5.730 elapsed time, the second fastest E.T. in history and the fastest ever in an elimination run.

It turned out he needed the blistering run because Bernstein was just a hair behind at 5.80.

Ricky Rudd moved into third place in the NASCAR point standings with a third place in the Northwestern Bank 400 at North Wilksboro, N.C. on April 8.

Rudd had led the 400-lap race with just 27 laps to go, but lost two places when he and the other leaders pitted during a flag. Kyle Petty finished fifth in his best performance of the young season.

One week later at the TranSouth 500 in Darlington, S.C., Bill Elliott proved he'd do anything to finish a race — even push his car across the line.

Elliott was running a comfortable third when his Coors'Melling Ford Thunderbird lost power in the next-to-last lap. He coasted to within 30 feet of the finish line and got out to push it the rest of the way as the crowd roared its approval.

# MAY

May started right when Californian John Bauer won the IMSA GTO race at Laguna Seca on May 6 in the Brooks Racing Ford Thunderbird.

Bauer not only won the race, but set a qualifying record of 101.405 mph and a GTO lap record of 102.620 mph in the 75-mile event.

Billy Meyer also had a record-breaking month in his 7-Eleven-sponsored Ford Mustang Funny Car, winning both an IHRA and an NHRA title within three weeks.

At the IHRA Pro-Am Nationals in Rockingham, N.C., May 7, Meyer set a national elapsed time record of 5.730 and ran a personal-best 255 mph in the Chief Auto Parts Mustang on his way to the title.

On May 27, Meyer was at it again, setting a track record E.T. of 5.814 on the way to beating Jim Head in the finals of the NHRA Cajun Nationals at Baton Rouge, La.

Buddy Baker in the Valvoline Ford Thunderbird took a thrilling third in the May 6 Winston 500 at Talladega, Ala., nipping two other drivers by inches in a photo finish.

In the rugged Mint 400 off-road race in Las Vegas on May 5, three Ford drivers had second-place finishes, Dave Shoppe (Class 8), Gale Pike (Class 3) and Willie Valdez (Class 7s).

On May 20, Mark Martin in a Ford Thunderbird won the ASA Coca Cola Badger 300 at the Slinger Speedway in Slinger, Wis. Martin dominated the 75-mile race, leading 218 of the 300 laps.

# JUNE

To say June was a successful month for Ford is putting it too mildly. Mercury Capri drivers completely dominated the SCCA Trans-Am circuit, and Bill Elliott finally scored his first NASCAR win of 1984.

The Capris started their victory splurge in the Motorcraft 100 on June 3 in Sonoma, Cal., with Greg Pickett in a Motorcraft Me4rcury Capri scoring a 5-second victory over Tom Gloy in a 7-Eleven-sponsored Capri.

Thirteen days later, Pickett and Gloy did it again, going 1-2 in the Portland Trans-Am. Pickett led all 53 laps and topped his Capri mate by 46 seconds.

But the highlight of the month was the Detroit Trans-Am through the streets of Motown on June 23.

Capri drivers made it look as easy as 1-2-3 with Gloy, Willy T. Ribbs (in his first 1984 Trans-Am) and Pickett snatching the top three spots, Gloy winning his first Trans-Am event since 1982.

In NASCAR, Bill Elliott gave his dad a Father's Day present to remember on June 17, winning the Miller High Life 400 at the Michigan International Speedway, the midway point race in the NASCAR season.

Elliott, who was fourth the week before at the Van Scoy Diamond Mine 500 in Long Pond, Pa., captured his first superspeedway win at MIS and only his second career win on the NASCAR circuit. He also set a record of 164.339 mph in qualifying for the pole position.

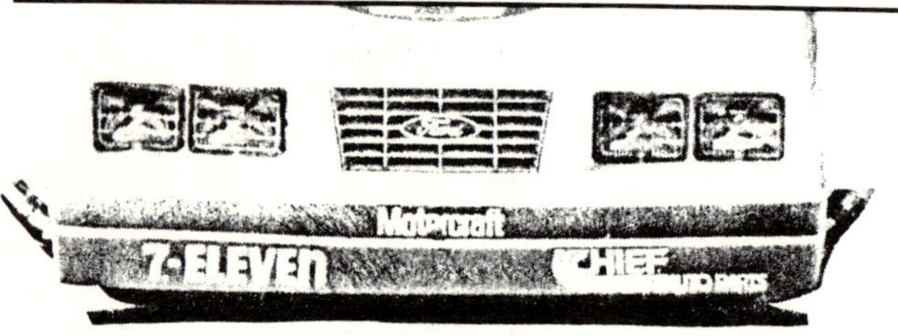


# JULY

The incredible Capri domination of the Trans-Am series continued right into July, reaching five consecutive victories.

At the Paul Revere 250 in Daytona, Fla. July 3, Mercury Capris finished 1-2 for the fourth consecutive time. Willy T. Ribbs, in only his second race for the Roush-Protofab team, took his first win of the season while Gloy finished in the runner-up position. Gloy, however, moved to the top of the point standings with his finish.

On July 22, Ribbs bested the field at the Pepsi Grand Prix weekend in Brainerd, Minn., also setting a race record with his 105.999 mph average. Gloy and Greg Pickett finished third and fourth, respectively.

On the drag racing scene, Billy Meyer won his fifth event in the last seven tries when he took the NHRA Molson Grandnational Funny Car title in Montreal on July 1. Bob Glidden took second in Pro Stock.

One week later at the Milan, Mich., IHRA Motorcraft Northern Nationals, Kenny Bernstein took the Funny Car title while Rickie Smith fought his way to a second in Pro Stock. Roy Hill set an IHRA world record in his Budget Car Rental Mercury Capri when he flew down the track at 189.07 mph.

On July 15 at the NHRA Summernationals in Englishtown, N.J., Bob Glidden scored his 40th career win in Pro Stock and Raymond Beadle took his first Funny Car win in 14 months when he topped Meyer in an all-Ford final.

Beadle, without a win for so long, took his second consecutive victory two weeks later at the NHRA Mile-High Nationals in Denver.

Willie Valdez and Dave Shoppe continued to win on the off-road circuit, both winning titles at the High Desert Fireworks 250 in Barstow, Cal. on July 7.

Then Stan Gilbert in a Ford F150 beat Shoppe and everyone else on July 28 to win the Class 8 title at the High Desert SNORE Midnight Special race.

Jeff Huber, driving a Chief Auto Parts-sponsored Ford Ranger, won one of the big stadium off-road races of the season on July 14, taking the Off-Road Championship Gran Prix in Indianapolis Hoosier Dome.

# AUGUST

John Bauer made infrequent appearances on the Camel GT circuit, but when he did appear, people couldn't help but remember what he did.

In only his second solo appearance of the season, Bauer roared to the Ford California GT title in GTO class, Aug. 5, setting qualifying and fastest lap records, again, in the superbly prepared Brooks Racing Thunderbird.

Tom Gloy stayed atop the Trans-Am standings with a second in the Aug. 5 Provimi Veal Trans-Am at Road America, then, two weeks later at historic Watkins Glen, N.Y., Willy T. Ribbs and Gloy battled to a 1-2 Capri finish in the Glen Trans-Am. It was Ribbs' third win in just five 1984 races.

In the IHRA Summernationals in Cincinnati, Ford drivers won two pro titles, Kenny Bernstein in Funny Car and Rickie Smith in Pro Stock.

On the NASCAR circuit, Bill Elliott set a qualifying record of 165.217 mph, then finished third in the Champion Spark Plug 400 at Michigan International Speedway, Aug. 12.

# SEPTEMBER

September, 1984, will be long remembered in Ford auto racing history.

The month started with the announcement that NASCAR great Cale Yarborough would be returning to the Ford fold in 1985, and it ended with the Capris clinching the first Trans-Am Manufacturer's Championship for Lincoln-Mercury Division and the first Trans-Am championship for Ford Motor Company since 1970.

Yarborough, who raced Fords from 1964 until Ford withdrew from the sport in 1970, announced he will race in 16 NASCAR races in 1985 in a new Ranier Racing Ford Thunderbird, scheduled to debut at Daytona in February.

The eagerly anticipated Trans-Am Manufacturer's Championship was clinched Sept. 23 at the Union Bay Sportswear Weekend in Seattle with yet another 1-2 Capri finish, Pickett edging Gloy.

A week later, the Capri contingent showed there would be no let-up after the championship when Pickett and Ribbs finished 1-2 in the Mercury Capri Fall Classic in Sonoma, Cal.

Billy Meyer set an IHRA world Funny Car record elapsed time of 5.628 at the IHRA Fall Nationals in Bristol, Tenn., Sept. 9, then won the IHRA's final event of the season, the U.S. Open Nationals in Rockingham, on Sept. 23.

At Rockingham, Rickie Smith and Roy Hill went 1-2 in an all-Ford Pro Stock final.

In SCORE off-road racing, Ford Ranger driver Chuck Johnson took a Class 7s win in the Off-Road World Championship, Sept. 16, at Riverside, Cal.

Lyn St. James, racing an Argo Ford in IMSA Camel GT events, established another milestone Sept. 30 in the IMSA New York 500 Camel GT. Her third-place marked the highest finish ever for a woman in Camel GT competition. St. James and co-driver Howdy Holmes, driving the Argo Ford, finished on the same lap as the winner of the 500-kilometer race.

## in '84

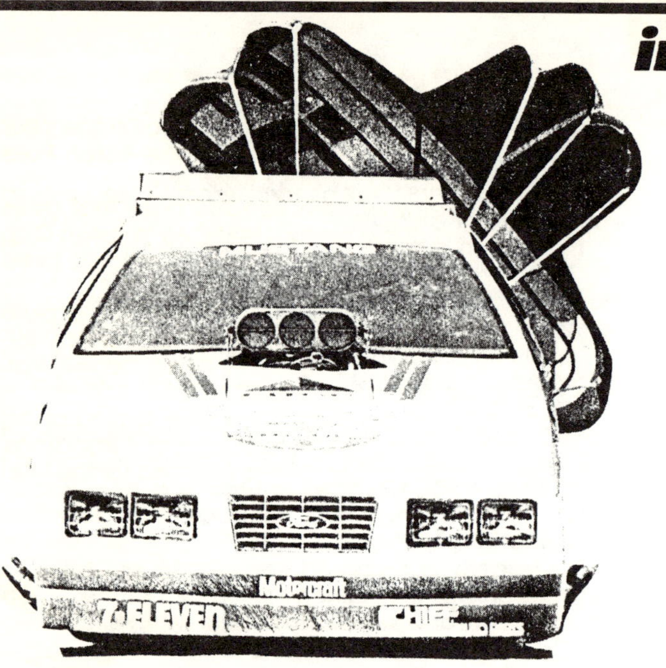


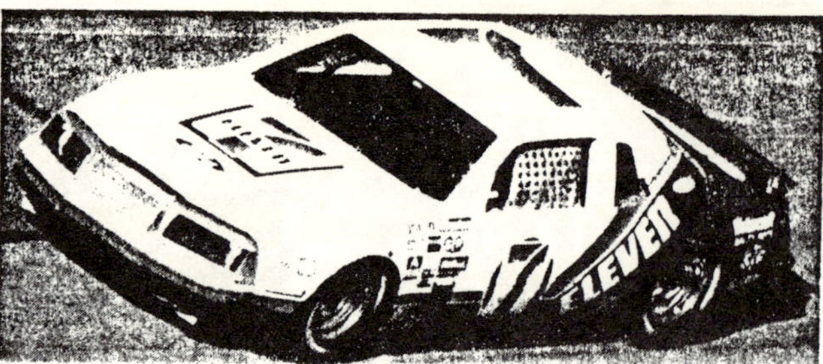


# OCTOBER

October belonged to Bill Elliott and Tom Gloy.

Elliott scored a pair of NASCAR Winston Cup victories, taking the Oct. 7 Miller High Life 500 in Charlotte, N.C., and the Oct. 21 Hodgdon American 500 in Rockingham, N.C.

Gloy clinched his first Trans-Am driver's title, Oct. 28 in the Texas Challenge race at Green Valley, although he was one of 15 (out of 23) drivers whose cars didn't survive the crash-marred race. Capris, for the ninth time, finished 1-2 with Willy T. Ribbs and Canadian rookie John Jones leading the field at Green Valley.

Ribbs' victory also assured a clean sweep for Capri drivers of the top three spots in the Trans-Am point standings, with Gloy, Greg Pickett and Ribbs guaranteed to finish 1-2-3.

Off the track, it was announced that the two first families of racing — the Pettys and Woods — would unite in 1985 under the Ford and 7-Eleven banners.

In a mock wedding ceremony at Charlotte Motor Speedway Oct. 2, Kyle Petty exchanged vows with Glen and Leonard Wood, describing the terms of their three-year contract.

Petty, who raced a 7-Eleven Ford Thunderbird in the 1984 season for Petty Enterprises, will race a 7-Eleven Thunderbird built and maintained by the Woods Brothers on the 1985 Winston Cup Grand National circuit.

Manny Esquerra and Willie Valdez continued to roar on the off-road circuit, both taking wins in the rugged High Desert Frontier 500 race in Las Vegas on Oct. 13.

Valdez, in his first attempt at a Frontier race, took the Class 7s race while Esquerra was tops in Class 7.

Bob Glidden added to his record victory total in October, driving his Pro Stock Ford Thunderbird to his 41st career win in the NHRA Winston World Series Final on Oct. 21 in Pomona, Cal.

At the same time, Glidden set a national elapsed time record of 7.61.

In the final point standings, Billy Meyer and Kenny Bernstein finished 2-3 in both the IHRA and NHRA Pro Funny Car standings while Rickie Smith was runner-up in the IHRA Pro Stock standings.

# NOVEMBER

Tom Gloy capped off what only can be described as an incredible year on the Trans-Am circuit at the Caesar's Palace Ford Motorcraft/Southland Trans-Am race on Nov. 11.

Gloy ended the year in style by winning the final race in record-breaking fashion, setting marks for fastest average winning speed of 88.82 mph and for fastest lap of 106.578 mph. The win capped a season in which he finished in the top five places in 14-of-16 starts (87.5 percent).

Willy T. Ribbs teamed with Wally Dallenbach Jr., in the Eastern Airline 3-Hour Camel GT race Nov. 25 at Daytona, driving a Roush Protofab Motorcraft Ford Mustang. They took first place in the GTO class and eighth overall in the combined GTO/GTP race.

As the off-road season also wound down, Willie Valdez secured a championship in Class 7s on the SCORE off-road circuit while Manny Esquerra and Dave Shoppe moved toward titles in Classes 7 and 8.

Both Esquerra and Shoppe scored class victories in the famed Baja 1000, Nov. 2. For Esquerra, it was his third Baja 1000 title in the last four years. Valdez finished second in Class 7s to clinch the title with one race to go.

# DECEMBER

Manny Esquerra in Class 7 and Dave Shoppe in Class 8 clinched SCORE off-road championships in the circuit's final race of the season, the Barstow (Cal.) Classic, Dec. 2, giving Ford trucks a sweep of SCORE titles.

Willie Valdez, who had already clinched the Class 7s title in November, ended the season with a victory at Barstow.

In December, the Ford Motor Company and Anheuser-Busch Inc., announced in Detroit the formation of a five-member Budweiser Motorcraft drag racing Superteam.

The Superteam is spearheaded by Funny Car ace Kenny Bernstein and Pro Stock star Frank Iaconio and includes Super Gas driver Larry Cummings, Super Stock racer Glen Tinsley and Competition Eliminator driver Jim Van Cleve, Jr.

Also in December, Bill Elliott capped off a fine year on the NASCAR circuit by winning the Busch Pole Award in the closest award chase ever.

Elliott, who received the $25,000 prize that goes with the award at the annual NASCAR Winston Cup award banquet in New York Dec. 7, edged three other drivers for the title.

The Ford driver piloted his Thunderbird to four pole positions during the season, a feat matched by fellow Ford Thunderbird driver Ricky Rudd, Darrell Waltrip and Cale Yarborough in 1984.

Elliott captured the award, however, based on his third-place finish in the Winston Cup point standings, the best finish of the four drivers who tied for the title.

# In Review: 1984-85 Performance Fords.

By Thomas E. Bonsall

There was a time, back in the freewheeling sixties, when Ford and high performance were practically synonymous. In almost every size category Ford built cars that led the industry in their ability to set the adrenalin flowing. All that ground slowly to a halt in the seventies under the combined weight of stringent safety, emissions and fuel standards. By the middle of the decade, there were those in Detroit who said that performance was gone for good; that it would never return...couldn't return. There were those in Detroit who even said the market no longer existed. Well, that latter view was certainly wrong-headed. There are as many high performance buffs out there as there always were, waiting for the metal merchants in Motown to get their act together and figure out how to build exciting cars within the limitations of the brave new world in which we now live. Ford engineers and designers, bless their hearts, have been doing just that. As a consequence, the last several years have been ones of increasingly satisfying news for Ford performance buffs.

The good news started with the introduction of the current Mustang platform in 1979. This car was available early-on in turbocharged form and is now offered in a couple of truly exciting formats. Primary among these have been the Mustang SVO and the Mustang GT. The SVO, a product of the Special Vehicles Operation at Ford, was first announced in 1984. The GT has been around for a few seasons, but for 1985 gets its own distinctive body parts (and therefore appearance) and a substantial increase in power. These two cars represent very different philosophies. It is rather remarkable, in fact, to find two cars as fundamentally removed from one another in personality coming out of the same car company. What happened was that two different sets of designers and engineers within Ford, each pursuing a coherent, but opposing, idea of what a high performance car should be, were given a relative free hand to bring their ideas to fruition.

The SVO is the very model of a modern, high-revving, high-tech performance car. The GT, on the other hand, harkens back to the straightforward performance ideas of the sixties. The SVO accomplishes its job with refinement and finesse; the GT blasts its way through with good old fashioned brute force. The SVO is a scalpel; the GT is a meat cleaver. As we said, two very different philosophies. The SVO may well be the wave of the future, but there are more than a few buffs out there (the author included) who will be sorry to see the lovable brutes disappear—if they do. The market for them has actually been growing stronger in recent years, and, if fuel economy standards can be met, the brutes could have a long life ahead of them, indeed.

The SVO, like the GT, sports its own external appearance package which, in the SVO's case, includes Ford's unique, dual polycarbonate rear spoiler. Up front is a functional hood scoop feeding into an intercooler. The SVO also uses a special louver behind the rear quarter windows that does a fairly good job of cleaning up the single least attractive aspect of this body shell.

Inside, in addition to full instrumentation, the SVO features articulated front bucket seats with center console and a slew of what in hardier times were considered luxuries—all as standard equipment: air conditioning, power windows, power door locks, tilt wheel, AM/FM stereo with tape deck and more. Missing from the list, and unavailable even as an option, is cruise control (an odd lapse considering the obvious effort to put together The Complete Driver's Car). Interior soft trim is available only in monotone charcoal, Ford's Color of the Decade for high performance vehicles. And they hope you like it. You might as well.

In terms of mechanicals, the heart of the SVO is the 2.3 liter, in-line 4-cylinder engine with port-injection and a turbocharger fitted with an air-to-air intercooler. Quoted horsepower is 175 at 4400 rpm.

The SVO chassis has been specially tuned for enthusiastic driving. Gas-filled Koni shocks are fitted in back, while gas-filled struts go up front. In general, the geometry has been completely revised and retuned. Brakes are discs on all four wheels, naturally, and 16-inch Goodyear radials are standard, as are cast aluminum wheels.

On the road, the SVO is comfortable, although not in the sybaritic way its standard features list would suggest. The goodies are there, of course, but the impression is of a thoroughly businesslike performance car, rather than a luxo-cruiser. The SVO is very fast, the turbo performance smooth and predictable. (This is in contrast to some other Ford systems—the Turbo T-Bird comes to mind—that are decidedly not.) The road holding ability is tremendous, too. The one flaw is a trick rear end. The SVO doesn't like slippery surfaces, whether wet or simply loose gravel. Unlike BMWs, which are notorious in this regard, the SVO gives the impression of being more stable than it is—until it lets go. More than one SVO has ended up in the weeds as a result. At least with the Bimmers you know you have to cut your speed 20 mph as soon as the first rain drop falls.

The GT features its own attractive exterior trim. Inside it is more luxurious—at least in appearance—than the SVO, with very comfortable, multi-tone articulated seats (available in charcoal or beige).

The main virtue of the GT is its 210 hp, 302 cid

V-8. Ford engineers have stuck with a four-barrel carb—as we said, this is your traditional musclecar. Braking is supplied by discs in front, drums in the rear and 15-inch wheels are used. In general, the chassis is a pretty straightforward, detuned version of that standard on the SVO, but it acquits itself in fine fashion. The standard five-speed manual shifter is super slick, with well-chosen gearing, and if your heart beats a little faster at the sound of a throbbing V-8 this car is a joy to run. The GT also comes as a convertible, so if that turns you on you can have your fun "al fresco," as it were.

During the test with the GT, the author had an unexpected opportunity to try (for the first time under duress) a space saver spare. The Mustang's radials were no match for the metal object about the size of a large screwdriver that found its way up through the tread and out the sidewall. A flat is never fun, but it is even less so during a winter storm. The puny-looking space saver spare, however, performed like a champ in the snow and ice. The traction was naturally somewhat compromised, but it fared about as well as a typical Detroit standard equipment tire. True, that may be no great shakes, but it is a darned sight better than used to be the case. Obviously improvements have been achieved in this area and Ford deserves credit for making emergency driving a little safer.

It is fascinating to compare the Mustangs to the Camaro Z-28 and Firebird Trans Am. Aesthetically, the GM twins are clearly more modern in appearance inside and out and, truth to tell, better lookers. The Mustangs aren't BAD looking; it is just that the General's boys are knockouts. The Trans Am, in particular,

**1985 Mustang GT**

**1984 Mustang SVO**

sets the standard for interior design in this league. The Z-28 is probably the best handler on a track. In the bump- and pothole-filled real world, however, the Z-28 is hard work—not nearly as friendly as the Mustangs or the Trans Am. For all-out, real world performance without spinal injury, the SVO probably takes first prize, with the GT and Trans Am being slightly cushier alternatives. In terms of overall quality, however, the Fords seem tighter. There have been lots of horror stories about GM quality control with the Camaro and Firebird, especially with the 1982 and 1983 models. The 1984s and 1985s are reportedly better, but Ford probably retains the title for best-built cars in this league. In fact, in all its lines, Ford Motor Company has been making real strides in quality control that some observers contend have put it ahead of the American competition, at least.

Bearing more than a family ressemblance to the Mustang, the current Thunderbird came along in 1983. It shares the Mustang platform and features Ford's new aerodynamic styling. Early T-Birds were compromised by cheap-looking interior door panels and instrument panels that were, quite simply, poorly designed. Full instrumentation was unavailable at any price, even on the Turbo. For 1985, those problems have been fixed with a vengeance and the T-Bird's interior now ranks with the best in the industry, especially at the higher trim levels.

The Turbo Coupe is the T-Bird of choice for enthusiasts. The main feature of interest is the overhead-cam, turbocharged 4-cylinder powerplant. On paper it looks like a more modern engine than the in-line four-banger available with the SVO, but the performance is inferior, primarily in power flow. The SVO's turbo is much smoother and has far less "turbo lag" than the T-Bird. The fact that the T-bird is heavier by several hundred pounds and has to make-do with 20 fewer horses may have something to do with it. Although the Turbo comes standard with a five-speed, it is more tractable and pleasant with the optional 3-speed automatic.

The whole character of the T-Bird seems more suited to the old V-8 school of high performance than to the high-revving turbo era. Ford tried to produce a sort of gentleman's SVO, but a T-Bird in the Mustang GT mold would have made for a more interesting car. Still, the Turbo Coupe in its black-out trim (new for 1985) and deluxe interior is a handsome, comfortable cruiser and there really isn't anything else much like it on the market.

The Pontiac 6000 STE, first announced in mid-1983, caused a considerable amount of attention to be paid to the idea of sport sedans and why America seems to be unwilling to make good ones in the European tradition. Well, the STE is a very good one, indeed, and in 1984, as a mid-year model, the LTD LX was trotted out to fly Ford's colors in that competition. One of the LX's prime virtues is that it is a couple of thousand dollars cheaper than the STE. Another, although a more subjective one, is the high output V-8 engine (the

STE comes with a six). The LX is the only sporty sedan in the world that can be had with a V-8. So, if you like that sort of thing, pay attention. In general, the LX has a lot of the feel of the Mustang GT (not entirely surprising considering they use the same basic platform and powerplant).

The LX features an upgraded LTD interior. Bucket seats and console are standard. The only available interior color is charcoal (surprise, surprise) and the outside trim is charcoal, as well. The suspension has been upgraded and cast aluminum 14-inch wheels are standard. The only transmission available is Ford's excellent 4-speed automatic overdrive. The slick 5-speed manual offered in the Mustang GT would increase the fun factor of the LX by a substantial margin. Another problem with the LX—and this is common to all high performance Fords—is the quietness of the exhaust. Most enthusiasts want to hear, as well as feel, the power, especially with a fire-breathing HO V-8. Ford engineers, however, have worked overtime to eliminate the V-8 rumble. At least in this reviewer's opinion, that is a major miscalculation. Nevertheless, the LX is a fun car to drive. The handling is far superior to anything Ford has ever put into an intermediate sedan and there are enough guts on demand to put it through its paces.

Another type of car Detroit has seemed singularly unable to build has been the compact sport sedan of the BMW 318i type. When Ford announced its Tempo compact in 1983 it seemed as far removed from that market as possible. It didn't have the power or the handling to compete—and didn't seem to care. In particular, the Tempo had possibly the worst 5-speed shift linkage in the industry, which rendered spirited driving an utter impossibility in any event.

Then a wondrous thing happened: the 1985 Tempo Sport GL. What Ford has done for 1985 is to put a high output four into the Tempo, mate it with a first-class 5-speed, tune up the chassis and throw in real seats. The result is a splendid little sport sedan—possibly the best this country has yet produced and at a price about half that of the 318i.

The heart of the Tempo Sport GL is the 2.3L+ 4-cylinder engine. This engine is a development of the 2.3 liter HSC (high swirl combustion engine) widely in use in Ford products. The idea was to offer the sort of performance formerly available only in overhead-cam powerplants of this size. The whole engine has undergone modifications and refinements, with new heads, manifolds, valve trains, air cleaners and so on. The bottom line is that this car really performs. And, it is not simply fast, either. As we noted above, the Sport GL is a well-rounded package that delivers in all areas, inside and out. With the proper promotion, Ford might have a real winner on its hands with this one.

**1984 Thunderbird Turbo**

Ford

1985 Tempo Sport GL

It is encouraging to see Ford so hard at work these days developing enthusiast-type vehicles. We knew they had it in them and pretty soon the whole automotive world (or at least that part that is paying attention with an open mind) should know, too. The Mustangs, SVO and GT, are the mainstays of the Ford performance stable, but there are other worthy contenders. The T-Bird Turbo Coupe is a fine gentleman's tourer. The LTD LX shows real promise and the new Tempo Sport GL is a truly exciting development.